ANATOMY & PH

MODEL ANSWERS

X 30441

Contents

Contents

Lymphatic System and Immunity

The Respiratory System

The Digestive System

The Urinary System

Reproduction and Development

For **important updates and errata**
please check the weblinks page:

www.thebiozone.com/weblink/AnaPhy-3572.html

The Biochemical Nature of the Cell (page 8)

1. (a) Golgi apparatus
   (b) Cytoplasm, mitochondria
   (c) Plasma membrane, vacuoles
   (d) Plasma membrane, vacuoles

2. Carbon, hydrogen, oxygen, nitrogen

3. Many examples acceptable:
   Calcium, structural component of bones and teeth, required for muscle contraction
   Iron, component of hemoglobin and cytochromes
   Sulfur, functional group of many coenzymes
   Phosphorus, component of phospholipids and nucleotides
   Potassium, intracellular ion, cell transport
   Chloride, component of extracellular fluid

Basic Cell Structure (page 9)

1. A generalized cell exhibits most of the characteristic features of a relatively unspecialized cell. It is not intended to represent any particular cell type but to illustrate features that collectively can be found in a range of cells.

2. (a) Phagocytiic white blood cell:
       Features: Engulfs bacteria and other foreign material by phagocytosis.
       Role: Destroys pathogens and other foreign material as well as cellular debris
   (b) Red blood cell (erythrocyte):
       Features: Biconcave cell, lacking mitochondria, nucleus, and most internal membranes. Contains the oxygen-transporting pigment, haemoglobin.
       Role: Uptake, transport, and release of oxygen to the tissues. Some transport of CO2. Lack of organelles creates more space for oxygen transport. Lack of mitochondria prevents oxygen use.
   (c) Rod cell of the retina:
       Features: Long, narrow cell with light-sensitive pigment (rhodopsin) embedded in the membranes.
       Role: Detection of light: light causes a structural change in the membranes and leads to a nerve impulse (result is visual perception).
   (d) Skeletal muscle cell:
       Features: Cylindrical shape with banded myofibrils. Capable of contraction (shortening).
       Role: Move voluntary muscles acting on skeleton.
   (e) Intestinal goblet cell:
       Features: Flask-shaped cell with basal nucleus and a cell interior filled with mucus globules.
       Role: Secrete mucus to protect the epithelium from abrasion and from the action of the enzymes involved in digesting the food.
   (f) Motor neuron:
       Features: Cell body with a long extension (the axon) ending in synaptic bodies. Axon is insulated with a sheath of fatty material (myelin).
       Role: Rapid conduction of motor nerve impulses from the spinal cord to effectors (e.g. muscle).
   (g) Spermatozoon:
       Features: Motile, flagellated cell with mitochondria. Nucleus forms a large proportion of the cell.
       Role: Male gamete for sexual reproduction. Mitochondria provide the energy for motility.
   (h) Osteocyte:
       Features: Cell with calcium matrix around it. Fingerlike extensions enable the cell to be supplied with nutrients and wastes to be removed.
       Role: In early stages, secretes the matrix that will be the structural component of bone. Provides strength.

3. Many cells are specialized to carry out a particular role and have organelles and structures specifically associated with that role, while lacking others that are not relevant or useful. For example, red blood cells lack a nucleus and most organelles, and are thus short lived, but this gives room inside the cell for them to carry a lot of hemoglobin, the oxygen-carrying pigment that enables them to fulfill their role in oxygen transport. Similarly, neutrophils have most organelles, (including many lysosomes), and are very mobile with the ability to engulf material. This is associated with their role of phagocytosis and destruction of foreign material.

The Structure of Membranes (page 11)

1. (a) Phospholipids are amphipathic, meaning they are molecules that are mostly lipid-like (hydrophobic) in structure, but at one end have a region that is polar or ionic (hydrophilic). The hydrophilic region is usually referred to as the head group, and the lipid portion is know as the tail(s). Because of this property, they tend to organize themselves into a bilayer so that the hydrophilic heads face outwards and the hydrophobic tails point in towards each other (away from the aqueous environment both outside and inside the cell).
   (b) This model accounts for the properties we observe in cellular membranes: its fluidity (how its shape is not static and how its components move within the membrane, relative to one-another) and its mosaic nature (the way in which the relative proportions of the membrane components, i.e. proteins, glycoproteins, glycolipids etc, can vary from membrane to membrane). The fluid mosaic model also accounts for how membranes can allow for the selective passage of materials (through protein channels for example) and how they enable cell-cell recognition (again, as a result of membrane components such as glycoproteins).

2. Membrane surface area is increased by the presence of microvilli and other types of surface projections.

3. (a) High surface area provides greater surface over which substances can move across and a greater surface area over which membrane-bound reactions can occur. This facilitates rapid transfers and more "reactive" surface area and increases the speed and efficiency of metabolic reactions.
   (b) Channel proteins and carrier proteins speed up the rates of diffusion into and out of the cell. Again, this facilitates rapid transfers and efficiency of function.

4. (a) Any of: Golgi apparatus, mitochondria, chloroplasts, endoplasmic reticulum (rough or smooth), nucleus, vacuoles, lysosomes, peroxisomes.
   (b) Depends on choice: Generally the membrane's purpose is to compartmentalize the location of enzymatic reactions, to control the entry and exit of substances that the organelle operates on, and/or to provide a surface for enzyme attachment.

5. Cholesterol lies between the phospholipids and prevents close packing, so it acts to regulate membrane fluidity.

6. (b) Tight junctions bind the membranes of neighboring cells, holding the cells together and making them impermeable to fluid and preventing molecules passing through the spaces between cells. Common in epithelia, e.g. the epithelia of the distal convoluted tubule in the nephron of the kidney, the epithelia of the lung, and the blood-brain barrier.
   (c) Desmosomes allow cell to cell adhesion to help resist shearing forces. Common in tissues subjected to mechanical stresses such as the simple and stratified squamous epithelium (e.g. skin cells).

7. Tight junctions are common where it is important that molecules (e.g. large proteins) do not leak between cells. Materials must actually enter the cells (by diffusion or active transport) in order to pass through the tissue. This pathway provides control over the entry of substances.

8. Labeled diagram:

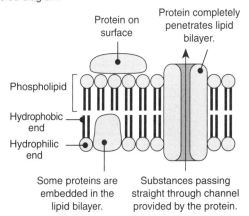

Protein on surface

Protein completely penetrates lipid bilayer.

Phospholipid

Hydrophobic end

Hydrophilic end

Some proteins are embedded in the lipid bilayer.

Substances passing straight through channel provided by the protein.

© 2009-2013 **BIOZONE** International
ISBN: 978-1-927173-59-6
Photocopying Prohibited

The Role of Membranes in Cells (page 13)

1. Membranes are critical to the functioning of cells. They form the outermost boundary of the cell and regulate the entry and exit of material into and out of the cell. They form the basis of membranous organelles involved in protein synthesis and packaging (rough ER), lipid and hormone synthesis (smooth ER), packaging and secretion (Golgi), and isolation of enzymes in compartments for cellular defense (peroxisomes, lysosomes). Membranes bind enzymes in a reaction sequence (as in the respiratory chain) or keep them together in a region where reactions occur (Krebs cycle enzymes). The components of membranes are also important in cellular recognition and communication.

2. (a) Golgi apparatus
   (b) Lysosome
   (c) Mitochondrion
   (d) Rough endoplasmic reticulum
   (e) Smooth endoplasmic reticulum
   (f) Peroxisome

3. Compartments within cells allow specific metabolic pathways in the cell to be localized. This achieves greater efficiency of cell function and restricts potentially harmful reactions and substances (e.g. hydrogen peroxide) to specific areas.

4. (a) Lipid soluble molecules pass easily through the phospholipid bilayer by dissolving in it. Lipid insoluble substances cannot pass directly into the bilayer (they must move through channels).
   (b) Lipid soluble substances pass very rapidly into cells (many drugs are lipid soluble). Lipid insoluble molecules must pass through protein channels by facilitated diffusion or active transport. The cell can't control the passage of lipid-soluble molecules moving down their concentration gradient

5. (a)-(c) Any of, in any order:
   – Oxygen
   – Energy source (=food = glucose)
   – Mineral and trace elements
   – Water

6. (a) Carbon dioxide   (b) Nitrogenous waste

Cell Structures and Organelles (page 15)

(b) **Name**: Mitochondrion
Location: In cytoplasm as discrete organelles
Function: Site of cellular respiration (ATP formation)
Visible under LM: Not with most standard school LM, but can be seen using high quality, high power LM.

(c) **Name**: Centrioles
Location: In cytoplasm, usually next to the nucleus.
Function: Involved in cell division (probably in the organization of the spindle fibers).
Visible under LM: No.

(d) **Name**: Ribosome
Location: Free in cytoplasm or bound to rough ER
Function: Synthesize polypeptides (=proteins)
Visible under LM: No

(e) **Name**: Golgi apparatus
Location: In cytoplasm associated with the smooth endoplasmic reticulum, often close to the nucleus.
Function: Final modification of proteins and lipids. Sorting and storage for use in the cell or packaging for export.
Visible under LM: Not with most standard school LM, but may be visible using high quality, high power LM.

(f) **Name**: Nucleus
Location: Discrete organelle, position is variable.
Function: The control center of the cell; the site of the nuclear material (DNA).
Visible under LM: Yes.

(g) **Name**: Endoplasmic reticulum (in this case, rough ER)
Location: Penetrates the whole cytoplasm. Continuous with the nuclear envelope.
Function: Involved in the synthesis of proteins for secretion, including sorting them to their destinations.
Visible under LM: No

(h) **Name**: Lysosome and vacuole (given)
Lysosome
Location: Free in cytoplasm.
Function: Ingests and destroys foreign material. Able to digest the cell itself under some circumstances.
Visible under LM: No
Vacuole (vacuole in an animal cell is shown).
Location: In cytoplasm.
Function: In animal cells, vacuoles are smaller and more numerous than in plant cells, and are involved in storage (of water, wastes, and soluble pigments).
Visible under LM: No in animal cells.

(i) **Name**: Cilia and flagella (given)
Location: Anchored in the cell membrane and extending outside the cell.
Function: Motility.
Visible under LM: Variably (depends on magnification and preparation/fixation of material).

(j) **Name**: Cellular junctions (given)
Location: At cell membrane surface, connecting adjacent cells
Function: Depends on junction type but basically cell adhesion and communication.
Gap junction: Act as communication channels between cells.
Tight junction: Prevent leakage of extracellular fluid from layers of epithelial cells.
Desmosome: Fasten cells together.
Visible under LM: No.

(k) **Name**: Cytoskeleton
Location: Throughout cytoplasm
Function: Provides structure and shape to a cell, responsible for cell movement (e.g. during muscle contraction), and provides intracellular transport of organelles and other structures.
Visible under LM: No

The Cell's Cytoskeleton (page 17)

1. They all enable movement.

2. Because it is dynamic, the cytoskeleton can move and change to alter cell shape, move materials around, and move the cell itself.

3. Materials being transported can be directed to their destination because they can move along specific cytoskeletal tracks which extend to specific parts of the cell.

Cell Processes (page 18)

1. (a) Golgi apparatus
   (b) Cytoplasm, mitochondria
   (c) Plasma membrane, vacuoles
   (d) Plasma membrane, vacuoles
   (e) Endoplasmic reticulum, ribosomes, nucleus
   (f) Chloroplasts
   (g) Centrioles, nucleus
   (h) Lysosomes
   (i) Plasma membrane, Golgi apparatus

2. (a) **Metabolism** describes all the chemical processes of life taking place inside the cell. Examples include cellular respiration, fatty acid oxidation, photosynthesis, digestion, urea cycle, and protein synthesis.
   (b) Catabolic: Digestion, cellular respiration, fatty acid oxidation. In these processes, larger molecules are being broken down to smaller ones, releasing stored energy.
   (c) Anabolic: Protein synthesis, photosynthesis, urea cycle. In these processes, smaller molecules are built up into larger, more complex ones, and are energy requiring.

Passive Transport Processes (page 19)

1. (a) Large surface area   (b) Thin membrane

2. (a) and (b) any of:
   – Molecules always move down a concentration gradient

© 2009-2013 **BIOZONE** International
ISBN: 978-1-927173-59-6
Photocopying Prohibited

(from high to low concentration).

- Molecules diffuse along their own concentration gradient, independent of other molecules.
- Diffusion rates are higher at higher temperatures.
- Diffusion rates are faster when the concentration gradient is greater.
- Thicker barriers slow diffusion.

3. (a) Channel-mediated facilitated diffusion, i.e through a protein channel in the membrane that creates a hydrophilic pore.
   (b) Carrier mediated facilitated diffusion, i.e. the molecule is aided across the membrane by a carrier protein specific to the molecule being transported.

4. Concentration gradients are maintained by constant use or transport away of a substance on one side of a membrane (e.g. use of ADP in mitochondria and by production of a substance on one side of a membrane (e.g. production of CO_2 by respiring cells).

5. Aquaporins are protein channels in the membrane specific to water molecules. This is faster (less resistance) than diffusion through the membrane.

6. (a) Hypotonic
   (b) Fluid replacements must induce the movement of water into the cells and tissues (which are dehydrated and therefore have a more negative water potential than the drink). **Note**: Many sports drinks are isotonic. Depending on the level of dehydration involved, these drinks are more effective when diluted.

7. (a) Water will move into the cells and they will burst (lyze).
   (b) The cells would lose water and the plasma membrane would crinkle up (crenulate).
   (c) Water will move into the cells and they will burst (lyze).

8. Malarial parasite: **Isotonic** to blood.

Ion Pumps (page 21)

1. ATP (directly or indirectly) supplies the energy to move substances against their concentration gradient.

2. (a) Cotransport describes coupling the movement of a molecule (such as sucrose or glucose) against its concentration gradient to the diffusion of an ion (e.g. H^+ or Na^+) down its concentration gradient. Note: An energy requiring ion exchange pump is used to establish this concentration gradient.
   (b) In the gut, a gradient in sodium ions is used to drive the transport of glucose across the epithelium. A Na^+/ K^+ pump (requiring ATP) establishes an unequal concentration of Na^+ across the membrane. A specific membrane protein then couples the return of Na^+ down its concentration gradient to the transport of glucose (at a rate that is higher than could occur by diffusion alone).
   (c) The glucose then diffuses from the epithelial cells of the gut into the bloodstream, where it is transported away. This maintains a low level in the intestinal epithelial cells.

3. Extracellular accumulation of Na^+ (any two of):
   - maintains the gradient that is used to cotransport useful molecules, such as glucose, into cells.
   - maintains cell volume by creating an osmotic gradient that drives the absorption of water
   - establishes and maintains resting potential in nerve and muscle cells
   - provides the driving force for several facilitated membrane transport proteins

Exocytosis and Endocytosis (page 22)

1. **Phagocytosis** is the engulfment of solid material by endocytosis whereas **pinocytosis** is the uptake of liquids or fine suspensions by endocytosis.

2. Phagocytosis examples (any of):
   • Feeding in *Amoeba* by engulfment of material using cytoplasmic extensions called pseudopodia. • Ingestion of

old red blood cells by Kupffer cells in the liver. • Ingestion of bacteria and cell debris by neutrophils and macrophages (phagocytic white blood cells).

3. Exocytosis examples (any of):
   • Secretion of substances from specialized secretory cells in multicellular organisms, e.g. hormones from endocrine cells, digestive secretions from exocrine cells. • Expulsion of wastes from unicellular organisms, e.g. *Paramecium* and *Amoeba* expelling residues from food vacuoles.

4. Any type of cytosis (unlike diffusion) is an active process involving the use of ATP. Low oxygen inhibits oxidative metabolism and lowers the energy yield from the respiration of substrates (ATP availability drops).

5. (a) **Oxygen**: Diffusion.
   (b) **Cellular debris**: Phagocytosis.
   (c) **Water**: Osmosis.
   (d) **Glucose**: Facilitated diffusion.

Mitosis and the Cell Cycle (page 23)

1. (a) The final chromosome status of a cell following mitosis is exactly the same as its parent. In contrast, a cell following meiosis has half the chromosome complement of the parent, i.e. it goes from diploid to haploid.
   (b) The biological role of mitosis is in growth, development, and repair of tissues, whereas the role of meiosis is to produce haploid gametes for the purposes of sexual reproduction.

2. Required answer in bold: The **DNA must be replicated** to form a second chromatid. The **chromosomes must condense** to avoid tangling.

3. A. Interphase: The stage between cell divisions (mitoses). Just before mitosis, the DNA is replicated to form an extra copy of each chromosome; still part of the same chromosome as an extra chromatid.
   B. Late prophase: Chromosomes condense (coil and fold up) into visible form. Centrioles move to opposite ends of the cell.
   C. Metaphase: Spindle fibers form between the centrioles. Chromosomes attach to the spindle fibers at the cell 'equator'.
   D. Late anaphase: Chromatids from each chromosome are pulled apart and move in opposite directions, towards the centrioles.
   E. Telophase: Chromosomes begin to unwind again. Two new nuclei form. A cleavage furrow forms across the midline of the parent cell, pinching it in two.
   F. Cytokinesis: Cell cytoplasm divides to create two distinct 'daughter cells' from the original cell. It is in this form for most of its existence, and carries out its designated role (normal function).

Control of the Cell Cycle (page 25)

1. If the cell cycle as not regulated, cell division could not be controlled. Cells would divide too early before they were large enough or had received appropriate signals from other cells, growth and development would be haphazard, chromosomal errors would be more likely, and cells could proliferate out of control, leading to tumors.

2. (a) Epithelial cells have a high turnover as they are constantly being replaced.
   (b) The cell cycle will shorten if there is damage to the tissue and it needs repair (rapid cell replacement).

Cancer: Cells out of Control (page 26)

1. Cancerous cells have lost control of the genetic mechanisms regulating the cell cycle so that the cells become immortal. They also lose their specialized functions and are unable to perform their roles.

2. The cell cycle is normally controlled by two types of gene: proto-oncogenes, which start cell division and are required for normal cell development, and **tumor-suppressor genes**,

© 2009-2013 **BIOZONE** International
ISBN: 978-1-927173-59-6
Photocopying Prohibited

which switch cell division off. Tumor suppressor genes will also halt cell division if the DNA is damaged and, if it cannot be repaired, will bring about a programmed cell suicide (apoptosis).

3. Normal controls over the cell cycle can be lost if either the proto-oncogenes or the tumor suppressor genes acquire mutations. Mutations to the proto-oncogenes, with the consequent formation of **oncogenes**, results in uncontrolled cell division. Mutations to the tumor-suppressor genes results in a failure to regulate the cell repair processes and a failure of the cell to stop dividing when damaged.

Levels of Organization (page 27)

1. (a) **Chemical**: Epinephrine (adrenaline), collagen, DNA, phospholipid, ATP.
   (b) **Organelles**: Lysosome, ribosomes, peroxisome.
   (c) **Cells**: Leucocyte, mast cell, neuron, Schwann cell, astrocyte.
   (d) **Tissues**: Blood, bone, cardiac muscle, cartilage, squamous epithelium.
   (e) **Organs**: Brain, heart, spleen, pancreas, liver, testis.
   (f) **Organ system**: Respiratory system, muscular system, nervous system, reproductive system.

2. Histology

Epithelial Tissues (page 28)

1. (a) The cells and associated extracellular substances (e.g. collagen).
   (b) Different tissues can be specialized for different tasks and within tissues different tasks can be shared amongst specialized cells. Every cell in every tissue does not have to perform every task so overall efficiency is greater.

2. Epithelial tissue forms the lining of internal and external body surfaces.

3. (a) Transitional epithelium has multiple layers (stratified) and is capable of stretching so it forms the protective lining of organs that regularly change in size (e.g. uterus, bladder).
   (b) Stratified epithelium has several layers so it is more durable than simple (single layered) epithelium and has a protective role where there is regular wear and tear, e.g. skin, vagina.

Muscle Tissue (page 29)

1. Summary below. Already completed cells in blue.
   Skeletal muscle:
   Appearance of cells: *Large, striated*
   Nuclei: Several per cell, peripheral
   Control: Voluntary

   Smooth muscle:
   Appearance of cells: Spindle shaped, non-striated
   Nuclei: *One central*
   Control: Involuntary

   Cardiac muscle:
   Appearance of cells: Striated. Short, branching fibers
   Nuclei: One, central
   Control: *Involuntary*

2. Skeletal muscle brings about voluntary (conscious) movement so its control is voluntary (innervated by motor neurons which terminate on the muscle fibers). The fibers are organized in an orderly fashion, with the contractile elements aligned to bring about coordinated contraction (and movement). In smooth muscle, the contractlie elements are more disorganized, so the muscle appears smooth and contractions are more diffuse and not coordinated as in skeletal muscle. Contraction is involuntary and the fibers are innervated by neurons of the autonomic nervous system. Cardiac muscle is a specialized striated muscle with branching fibers containing orderly contractile elements and a large number of mitochondria (required to maintain aerobic metabolism without fatigue). Contraction of the cardiac muscle cells is involuntary and no external innervation is required to initiate the heart beat. The cells are electrically coupled through specialized intercalated disks so that the heart beats in a coordinated fashion.

Connective Tissues (page 30)

1. (a) Most common cell type: **fibroblasts**.
   (b) Role: synthesize collagen and extracellular matrix.
   (c) Common fiber type: **collagen**.

2. Connective tissues are the supporting tissues of the body and may be very hard (bone), tough but flexible (tendon), or fluid (blood). Dense CTs occur where strength is needed (e.g. ligaments and tendons). Loose CTs are less dense and occur around internal organs, anchoring them in place and supporting them. Special CTs are specialized for particular functions. Bone is very hard and forms the hard parts of the skeleton. Cartilage is more flexible than bone and forms the supporting structures of the skeleton, e.g. on the ends of bones where they form joints). Blood is a liquid tissue and the formed elements (the cells) are supported in a fluid matrix, which transports material around the body. Adipose tissue (another specialized CT) stores fat.

Nervous Tissue (page 31)

1. (a) Densely packed neurons with associated supporting cells. In the CNS, gray matter (cell bodies) and white matter (axons) can be seen.
   (b) Role of glial cells: provide physical and metabolic support for the neurons, i.e they surround neurons and hold them in place, and supply nutrients and oxygen to the neurons.
   (c) The cerebrospinal fluid is a nutritive fluid (i.e. it supplies oxygen and nutrients to the neural tissue). It is circulated through the ventricles of the brain and the central canal of the spinal cord.

2. Neural tissue is responsible for receiving and responding to stimuli. The sensory structures and sense organs are made up of neural tissue and they receive stimuli and send messages to a central processing point in the central nervous system. The CNS coordinates an appropriate response, e.g. a muscle contraction or secretion from a gland.

Human Organ Systems (page 35)

1. Muscular system: movement of body (limbs, locomotion), and its component parts (e.g. gut).

2. Skeletal system: support and protection of tissues and organs, movement (with muscular system), production of blood cells.

3. Integumentary system: physical and chemical protection of tissues, thermoregulation, synthesis of vitamin D precursor.

4. Urinary system: excretion of nitrogenous wastes, toxins, and other metabolic waste products. Maintenance of fluid and electrolyte balance.

5. Digestive system: physical and chemical digestion and absorption of ingested food to provide the body's fuel.

6. Nervous system: regulates all visceral and motor functions of the body.

7. Reproductive system: production of gametes and offspring.

8. Respiratory system: Interface for gas exchange with the internal environment - obtaining oxygen and expelling CO_2.

9. Lymphatic system: circulates tissue fluid, internal defense against pathogens.

10. Cardiovascular system: delivers oxygen and nutrients to all tissues and organs and removes CO_2 and other waste products of metabolism.

© 2009-2013 **BIOZONE** International
ISBN: 978-1-927173-59-6

11. Endocrine system: produces hormones that activate and regulate homeostatic functions, growth, and development. Primary components:

Hypothalmus (nervous and endocrine function secretes oxytocin and ADH as well as releasing hormones, which regulate the hormones of the anterior pituitary.

Pituitary: secretes hormones to regulate the activities of other endocrine glands.

Parathyroid glands: secrete PTH for regulation of blood calcium.

Pancreatic islets: secrete hormones to regulate carbohydrate metabolism.

Testes (male) secrete testosterone for maintaining maleness and for sperm production.

Ovaries secrete estrogen and progesterone to maintain femaleness, control the menstrual cycle, and prepare for and maintain pregnancy.

Pineal secretes melatonin to regulate the sleep-wake cycle.

Adrenal glands secrete corticosteroids for regulating aspects of sodium regulation and responses to stress.

KEY TERMS: Mix and Match (page 33)

active transport (E), cell (DD), cellular differentiation (L), chromosome (AA), connective tissue (U), cytokinesis (B), diffusion (T), endocytosis (C), epithelial tissue (J), exocytosis (V), hypertonic (W), hypotonic (A), interphase (M), ion pump (R), isotonic (BB), metaphase (O), mitosis (S), muscle tissue (P), nervous tissue (H), organ (N), organ system (D), organelle (G), osmosis (Y), partially permeable membrane (K), passive transport (Q), phospholipid (F), prophase (I), telophase (Z), tissue (CC).

Principles of Homeostasis (page 35)

1. **Receptors** (detect stimuli), **control and coordination center** (integration of signals and coordination of response), **effectors** (implement an appropriate response).

2. Negative feedback mechanisms enable maintenance of a steady state internal environment despite fluctuations in the external environment (e.g. rising air temperature). Negative feedback mechanisms are self-correcting so that physiological systems are stabilized against excessive change.

Positive Feedback (page 36)

1. (a) Positive feedback has a role in accelerating a physiological process to bring about a particular required response. Examples include (1) elevation in body temperature (fever) to accelerate protective immune responses, (2) positive feedback between estrogen and LH to leading to an LH surge and ovulation, (3) positive feedback between oxytocin and uterine contractions: oxytocin causes uterine contraction and stretching of the cervix, which causes more release of oxytocin and so on until the delivery of the infant.

(b) Positive feedback is inherently unstable because it causes an escalation in the physiological response, pushing it outside the tolerable physiological range. Compare this with negative feedback, which is self correcting and causes the system to return to the steady state.

(c) Positive feedback loops are normally ended by a resolution of situation causing the initial stimulation. For example, the positive feedback loop between estrogen and LH leading to ovulation is initiated by high estrogen levels and ended when these fall quickly after ovulation, prompting a resumption of negative feedback mechanisms. In childbirth, once the infant is delivered, the stretching of the cervix ceases and so too does the stimulation for more oxytocin release.

(d) When positive feedback continues unchecked, it can lead to physiological collapse. One example includes unresolved fever. If an infection is not brought under control (e.g. by the body's immune system mechanisms or medical intervention), body temperature will continue to rise and can lead to seizures, neurological damage, and death.

Body Membranes and Cavities (page 37)

1. (a) A=parietal pleura
   (b) B=visceral pleura
   (c) C=visceral pericardium
   (d) D=parietal pericardium

2. (a) Epithelial membranes (the skin, mucosa, and serosa) line, protect, and in some cases lubricate the surfaces of the body. They may be dry (as in skin) or absorptive or secretory.
   (b) Synovial membranes are composed of connective tissue only and contain no epithelial cells. Epithelial membranes, as the name suggests, are formed from epithelial and connective tissue.

3. (a) Serous membranes occur in pairs to separate the organs in a cavity from the body wall (e.g. one serous membrane lines the organ and one lines the body wall. The space between the membranes forms a cavity that reduces friction.
   (b) The serous fluid lubricates the organs and reduces friction as body parts move (e.g. during breathing.

4. (a) Mucosa (muscous membrane).
   (b) The skin (cutaneous membrane) is not thin and bathed in watery secretions, but thick and dry and open to the air. It thus provides protection against drying out, and physical, chemical and bacterial damage. If it was a moist membrane, too much water would be lost to the environment.

Maintaining Homeostasis (page 39)

1. Two mechanisms operating to restore homeostasis after infection ((a) and (b) any two of):
   - Immune system response with the production of antibodies against the antigens of the pathogen (humoral response).
   - Immune system response with the production of T cells which recognize the antigens of the pathogen and destroy them directly (cell-mediated response).
   - Local inflammatory response (redness, pain, swelling, heat) at the site of infection.
   - Fever (widespread increase in body temperature).
   - The production of antimicrobial substances like interferon and interleukin-1.
   - Phagocytosis of pathogen by white blood cells. All the above aim to destroy the pathogen and/or its toxins and assist a return to homeostasis.

For Q. 2.-4., more detail is given than may be required.

2. Mechanisms by which responses to stimuli are brought about and coordinated:
   (a) **Hormonal response** to stimuli: Endocrine glands respond to a stimulus (e.g. a nerve impulse or another hormone or metabolite) by producing hormones which bring about an appropriate physiological response. **For example**, nervous stimulation of the adrenal glands when the body receives a stressful stimulus causes the release of epinephrine. This hormone causes mobilization of glucose in muscle and liver cells, increases heart rate and directs blood away from nonessential organs. These responses help the body react to the stress situation.
   (b) **Nervous response** to stimuli: Direct stimulation of nerves from a sensory receptor causes a reaction to the stimulus. This may be a response requiring interpretation of the message by the brain or it may be a reflex (an automatic response to a stimulus involving only 2 or 3 neurons), e.g. pain withdrawal.

3. Maintaining water and ion balance by:
   (a) Water and ions are taken in with food and drink, helping to replace that lost through urine, faeces, and sweat. The digestive organs and all of the digestive hormones (e.g. amylase in the mouth, pepsin in the stomach, trypsin in the small intestine) are all involved in breaking down food and facilitating absorption into the bloodstream.
   (b) The kidney is the primary regulator of fluid and ions. When large quantities of fluid must be excreted, the kidney produces large amounts of dilute urine. When water must be conserved, small amounts of concentrated urine are produced. ADH (antidiuretic hormone) causes more water to be reabsorbed from

the kidney (causing a more concentrated urine). ADH increases when blood water levels are low. Essential ions (and glucose) are retained by active reabsorption from the kidney tubules. Another hormone, aldosterone from the adrenal glands, increases the absorption of sodium ions.

Note: Water and ions are lost via sweat and water is lost in breathing. These losses are compensated for by the homeostatic role of the kidney. Sweating is a mechanism for thermoregulation. It is not usually an major way to rid the body of excessive water and salts.

4. Regulating respiratory gases during exercise by:
    (a) **Increasing breathing rate**. This increases both the rate of oxygen entering the lungs and the rate at which carbon dioxide leaves. It also increases the rate of loading and unloading of oxygen and carbon dioxide into and out of the bloodstream.
    (b) **Increasing the heart rate**. This increases blood flow which facilitates the loading and unloading of oxygen and carbon dioxide into and out of the bloodstream. It also increases the speed of delivery of oxygen to working tissues (e.g. muscles) and speeds up the removal of carbon dioxide and other waste products of metabolism.

Diagnostic Medicine (page 41)

1. (a) A CT scan uses a series of X-rays to reconstruct a 3-D image of a tissue or organ. This image can be used to detect abnormalities such as tumors.
    (b) MRI uses computer analysis of high frequency radio waves (passed through tissue) to map out variations in tissue density.

2. Computer imaging techniques are non-invasive (unlike surgery) and can give an accurate cross-sectional picture of an area of the body for the detection of tumors and other abnormalities in tissues. They are particularly useful in areas where other techniques are unsuitable (e.g. the central nervous system).

3. Whereas X-rays pass **through** a person and expose photographic film, radionuclide scanning involves the introduction of the radionuclide **into** the body where it is differentially absorbed by different tissues. These tissues then emit radiation which is detected by a gamma camera.

4. Endoscopy allows exploration of organs and tissues without extensive surgery. This is useful for diagnosing the exact nature and location of problems (e.g. blocked fallopian tubes or roughened areas of cartilage in a knee joint). **Explanatory note**: Once a problem is diagnosed, surgery can be performed if necessary, using very small incisions and specialized surgical tools that cause minimal tissue damage (endoscopes are used for viewing during the surgery).

5. Biosensors use biological material, e.g. an enzyme, to detect the presence or concentration of a substance. The biological material is immobilized within a semi-conductor. Its activity (response), causes an ion change which is detected by a transducer, amplified, and displayed as a read-out.

The Integumentary System (page 43)

1. (a) and (b) any of in any order:
    - Thermoregulation: cooling by sweating, vasodilation, and hair flattening, conserving heat by vasoconstriction and hair erection.
    - Skin contains sensory receptors to enable appropriate responses to pain, pressure, heat etc.
    - Skin secretes sebum and antimicrobial substances to protect against microbial invasion.
    - Skin contains melanocytes which provide protection against excessive UV light.
    - Skin absorbs UV light and produces a vitamin D precursor (needed for calcium absorption).

2. A tattoo inserts ink into the upper layer of the dermis where it becomes trapped within fibroblasts (as part of the body sealing off the foreign material). While it is trapped here, it remains an inert and permanent component of the skin.

3. (a) Stratum basale: Epidermis (innermost). The

regenerative layer of cells, which produces new cells and also contains the mealnocytes, which give skin its protective dark pigment.
    (b) Stratum corneum: Epidermis (outermost). Provides protection against wear and therefore protects the deeper layers of cells.
    (c) Sweat glands: Dermis (reticular layer): Produce sweat, which cools by evaporation (thermoregulation).
    (d) Collagen fibers: Lower dermis. Provide strength to the dermis, making it resilient.

Thermoregulation (page 45)

1. Body temperature reduced by (a and b any two of):
    • Sweating (cooling by evaporation) • Reducing activity • Behavioral mechanisms such as removing clothing or seeking shade • Increasing blood flow to skin (increases radiation from the skin surface).

2. (a) **Hypothalamus**: Monitors temperature changes in the body and coordinates appropriate responses to counteract the changes.
    (b) **Skin**: Detects changes in skin temperature and relays the information to the hypothalamus. In response to input from the hypothalamus, muscles and capillaries in the skin act as effectors to bring about an appropriate thermoregulatory response.
    (c) **Nervous input to effectors**: (from hypothalamus) brings about (through stimulation of muscles) an appropriate thermoregulatory response (e.g. raising hairs, constricting blood vessels).
    (d) **Hormones**: Mediate a change in metabolic rate through their general action on body cells (epinephrine and thyroxine increase metabolic rate).

3. (a) Sweating cools by evaporation. As high energy evaporate from the skin, they release energy absorbed from the body.
    (b) Alcohol evaporates at a lower temperature than water (more volatile) so evaporates very quickly, causing a sensation of cold.

4. Changes in body temperature (skin or core) are detected by the hypothalamus which coordinates counteracting responses via the autonomic system (sympathetic and parasympathetic branches). The changes are regulated through negative feedback.

5. When the blood vessels in the skin constrict (diameter becomes smaller), blood flow to the skin is reduced and blood is kept near the body's core to retain heat. When the blood vessels dilate, blood flow to the skin increases and heat is lost from the skin's surface.

6. A person from a cool climate would have lost the activity of many of their sweat glands. When they visit a hot climate, the remaining sweat glands have to cope with trying to cool the body, and the amount of sweat they produce and the way it is distributed is insufficient to comfortably cope with the job.

Hypothermia (page 47)

1. Exposure to low temperatures even for a short time without insulation will lead to hypothermia. Even temperatures of 15 to 20°C may cause hypothermia if a person is exposed long enough without protection. Exposure to water will cause hypothermia far more quickly than the same temperature in air as heat is more easily conducted away from the body.

2. (a) Short and stocky
    (b) A short, stocky shape has a lower SA:V ratio and so loses heat more slowly.

3. Methods include passive rewarming (using a person's own body heat) for mild hypothermia, active external rewarming (using external heating) for moderate hypothermia and active internal rewarming (using devices to warm body fluids internally) for severe hypothermia. Using an incorrect method may cause premature dilation of blood vessels and so cause a reduction in blood pressure as well as a further drop in body temperature.

© 2009-2013 **BIOZONE** International
ISBN: 978-1-927173-59-6
Photocopying Prohibited

Hyperthermia (page 48)

1. (a) Hyperthermia is the condition in which the core body temperature rises without a rise in the body's set-point temperature.
   (b) During a fever, the body's set-point temperature is elevated by the hypothalamus.

2. (a) Shivering is a mechanism that produces heat, thus heat loss would actually be slowed.
   (b) Core body temperatures above 40°C will rapidly lead to death if not treated. Internal cooling allows rapid reduction of the core temperature.

3. Untreated heat stroke leads to death because the excessive internal core temperature causes metabolic reactions to stop working as enzymes denature.

Drugs and Thermoregulation (page 49)

1. (a) Ecstasy causes an increase in body temperature in rabbits. There is a positive relationship between the ecstasy dose and the increase in body temperature.
   (b) Ecstasy decreases blood flow to the skin of rabbits. There is a negative relationship: as ecstasy dose increases, blood flow to the skin decreases.

2. Ecstasy causes a number of physiological effects that increase body temperature. It causes vasoconstriction of the blood vessels, limiting the amount of blood flow to the skin. This reduces the body's ability to cool down, and results in an increased core temperature. It also increases metabolic rate, which generates additional heat. Ecstasy may also inhibit feelings of thirst, so people do not feel the need to drink. Sweat production is reduced, so the body's ability to cool itself down is further reduced.

Homeostasis in Newborns (page 50)

1. Newborns cannot shiver, and have limited capacity to generate internal heat from large muscle movements. They have very large body surface area compared to their volume, a large number of blood vessels that run close to the skin surface, and only a small amount of fat for insulation.

2. Constricting blood vessels close to the skin reduces heat loss from the core to the extremities. Dilating the skin's blood vessels directs excess heat to the extremities and heat is lost to the environment.

3. Newborns are at risk of dehydration because they can't concentrate urine. Thus they lose a large volume of water through urine, which must be replaced.

KEY TERMS: Mix and Match (page 51)

abdominal cavity (V), anterior/ventral (R), dermis (P), distal (E), dorsal body cavity (B), epidermis (I), epithelial membranes (O), homeostasis (C), hypodermis (M), inferior (G), lateral (D), mucous membranes (K), negative feedback (S), pelvic cavity (W), positive feedback (L), posterior/dorsal (A), proximal (X), serous membranes (serosa) (F), superficial (N), superior (Q), synovial membranes (H), thoracic cavity (T), ventral body cavity (J).

The Human Skeleton (page 55)

1. (a) Scapula
   (b) Humerus
   (c) Rib
   (d) Lumbar vertebra
   (e) Ilium
   (f) Sacrum
   (g) Carpals
   (h) Metacarpals
   (i) Phalanges
   (j) Tibia
   (k) Tarsals
   (l) Metatarsals
   (m) Cranium
   (n) Facial bones
   (o) Clavicle
   (p) Sternum
   (q) Femur
   (r) Patella
   (s) Fibula
   (t) Phalanges

2. Limb girdles (1) attach the limbs to the axial skeleton and (2) enable the limbs to move freely.

3. (a) To allow passage of the infant's head through the pelvis during childbirth.
   (b) To allow for rapid early growth of the brain.

4. Foramina allow nerves and blood vessels supplying the tissues above and below the skull to pass through the bone.

5. (a) Parietal.   (b) Temporal bone.

6. Patella is a short bone.

7. (not 6) parietal is a flat bone.

8. (not 7) Domed skull forms a protective bony enclosure for the brain.

9. (not 8) Facial bones hold the eyes in position and enable attachment of the facial muscles.

10. (not 9) Talking, laughing, or singing.

The Bones of the Spine (page 57)

1. (a) Lumbar vertebrae
   (b) Thoracic vertebrae
   (c) Atlas (cervical 1)
   (d) Cervical vertebra
   (e) Sacrum

2. S shape brings center of mass to the mid-line of the body. (Explanatory note: This gives the best mechanical advantage in terms of least muscular effort to stand upright and least force on spinal joints).

3. The extra bones are fused into single bones.

The Limb Girdles (page 58)

1. (a) Shoulder girdle connects the upper limbs and the axial skeleton on each side of the body.
   (b) The sternoclavicular joints (between sternum and clavicle) on each side.

2. Bones are large and thick, and also fused together providing strength and rigidity to help support weight of the body. The bowl shape helps to retain the organs of the abdominal cavity and provides protection for the reproductive organs in particular.

3. The female pelvis is larger and broader than the male pelvis which is taller, narrower, and more compact. The female inlet (space between the bones) is also larger and oval, whereas the male's is more heart-shaped). These differences are associated with accommodating the passage of the infant's head during childbirth.

4.

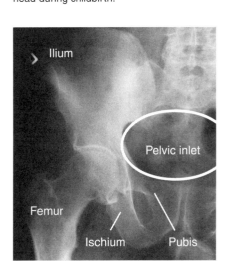

© 2009-2013 **BIOZONE** International
ISBN: 978-1-927173-59-6
Photocopying Prohibited

Bone (page 59)

1. Bones grow in length by continuous growth of new cartilage in the epiphyseal plate, which is then covered in a bone matrix and calcified to form new bone. Appositional growth, in contrast, involves addition of new bone to the outside of the diaphysis and resorption of bone from the inner diaphysis surface.

2. (a) Support: Provides a frame to keep the body supported.
   (b) Protection: Bones can serve to protect internal organs, such as the skull protecting the brain or the ribs protecting the heart and lungs.
   (c) Movement: Bones, skeletal muscles, tendons, ligaments, and joints function together to generate and transfer forces so that body parts or the whole body can be moved.
   (d) Blood cell production: The marrow, located within the medullary cavity of long bones and interstices of cancellous bone, produces blood cells in a process called haematopoiesis.
   (e) Mineral storage: Bones act as reserves of minerals important for the body, most notably calcium and phosphorus.

3. (a) Epiphyseal plate
   (b) Diaphysis
   (c) Periosteum
   (d) Epiphysis

The Ultrastructure of Bone (page 61)

1. Osteoblasts are the active bone-producing cells. Osteocytes are mature osteoblasts and maintain the bone, rather than create it.

2. See image at the top of the next column.

3. The Haversian canals contain the blood vessels and nerves so that wastes can be removed from the bone tissue and the bone cells can be supplied with oxygen, nutrients, and sensory information.

4. (a) Dense bone has a regular arrangement of repeating units or osteons. Spongy bone has a less regular structure, with large spaces filled with red bone marrow.
   (b) Spongy bone is more likely to become brittle because it has a looser structure with holes, so any loss of mass will make the holes larger and the bone more inclined to fracture.

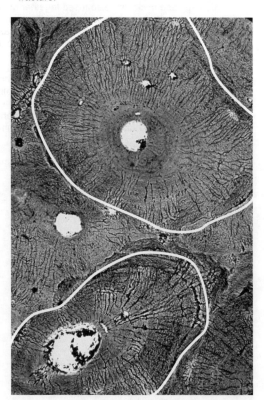

Joints (page 62)

1. Joints allow movement of the skeleton, which is otherwise rigid.
2. Bones are held together at joints by tough (but flexible) connective tissue structures called ligaments.

Synovial Joints (page 63)

1. Question should say joint models (A-E) **above**:
   (a) Pivot - B
   (b) Hinge - D
   (c) Ball and socket - E
   (d) Saddle - A
   (e) Gliding - C

2. (a) Question should read: What features **are** common to most synovial joints?
   Synovial joints have a joint capsule separating the bone articulating bones, which contains synovial fluid (secreted by the synovial membranes). They allow free movement in one or more planes and are usually reinforced by ligaments.
   (b) Synovial fluid reduces friction between the articular cartilage and other tissues in joints to lubricate and cushion them during movement. The cartilage lines the bone ends and provides the resistance to load and shock.

3. (a) The ligaments of the knee joint prevent excessive rotation and lateral movements while allowing flexion and extension (the normal action of the knee ending and unbending).
   (b) During sporting activity, twisting caused by falls or collisions, produces sudden excessive torsional forces on the ligaments normally supporting the alignment and normal action of the knee joint.
   (c) Torn ligaments (and tendons) are slow to heal because of their poor blood supply (blood delivers oxygen and nutrients to speed healing). Joints are also moved constantly so the ligaments can stay under strain unless immobilized (which itself slows healing).

Aging and Diseases of the Skeleton (page 65)

1. Age-related loss of bone mass is the result of a slowing in the rate of bone remodeling; rates of bone loss exceed rates of bone deposition as cell renewal rates slow.

2. (a) An osteoarthritic joint loses cartilage and synovial fluid and the bone wears, causing the joint to stiffen and become less mobile.
   (b) The loss of cartilage and bone at the joint leads to tissue inflammation, which causes pain.

3. The weight-bearing joints take most of the body's weight so are eroded more quickly by the higher loads they carry.

4. (not 3) Mechanical stress on the joint is behind OA and repetitive actions and joint injuries add to the sum of mechanical stresses on a joint.

5. (not 4) The density of minerals in bone is what gives bone its strength. With a loss of the mineral matrix, the bone becomes more porous and weaker, and so more inclined to fracture.

6. (not 5)
   (a) Male 40%   (b) Female 50%.

7. (not 6) calcium is important when bone is being made and a large proportion of a person's total bone density is laid down in the first 20 years. Calcium intake from diet should not be inadequate during this time.

8. (not 7) Bone remodeling allows bone to be reshaped and repaired and it occurs in response to the normal stress of weight-bearing activity. Without physical activity, less bone remodeling occurs, and bone losses are not replaced as effectively, if at all.

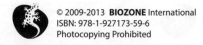
© 2009-2013 **BIOZONE** International
ISBN: 978-1-927173-59-6
Photocopying Prohibited

KEY TERMS: Mix and Match (page 67)

appendicular skeleton (M), axial skeleton (G), bone (tissue) (J), cartilage (Y), artilaginous joint (Q), compact (=cortical) bone (T), fibrous joint (O), flat bones (C), Haversian canals (A), irregular bones (P), joint (articulation) (B), ligament (W), long bones (D), matrix (of bone) (U), ossification (Z), osteoarthritis (R), osteoblasts (I), osteocyte (V), osteroporosis (L), parathyroid hormone (X), pectoral girdle (F), pelvic girdle (S), periosteum (E), synovial fluid (H), synovial joint (N), tendon (K).

Muscles of the Human Body (page 69)

1. (a) Facial muscles
    (b) Deltoid
    (c) Trapezius
    (d) Pectorals
    (e) Triceps
    (f) Biceps
    (g) Latissimus dorsi
    (h) Obliques (abdominal group)
    (i) Gluteals
    (j) Rectus abdominis (abdominal group)
    (k) Hamstrings
    (l) Quadriceps
    (m) Gastrocnemius

2. (a) Calf muscles (gastrocnemius and soleus)
    (b) Quadriceps (a group of four muscles)
    (c) Biceps (biceps brachii) helped by the supinator/pronator in the forearm (contrary to what most people think, the biceps main function is not to flex the forearm but to rotate it).
    (d) Deltoid

    It helps to perform these actions when working out what muscle groups are involved!

3. The facial muscles have their origin on bone but are inserted into soft tissues (e.g. skin), rather than into another bone.

4.

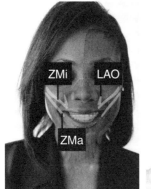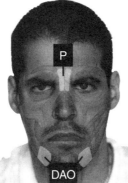

5. In parallel muscles, the fascicles run parallel to the long axis of the muscle (the axis of force generation) whereas in a fusiform muscle (a subcategory of parallel muscles) the muscle is wider and shaped like a cylinder in the middle, tapering at the ends (i.e. spindle-shaped). The force a fusiform muscle generates is concentrated in a smaller area.

Skeletal Muscle Structure and Function (page 71)

1. The neuromuscular junction is specialized cholinergic synapse formed where a motor neuron terminates on the sarcolemma (plasma membrane) of a muscle fiber. It consists of the axon terminal (synaptic end bulb) and the region of the sarcolemma it makes contact with.

2. (a) The banding pattern results from the overlap pattern of the thick and thin filaments (dark = thick and thin filaments overlapping, light = no overlap).
    (b) **I band**: Becomes narrower as more filaments overlap and the area of non-overlap decreases.
    H zone: Disappears as the overlap becomes maximal (no region of only thick filaments).
    Sarcomere: Shortens progressively as the overlap becomes maximal.

3. They protect the muscle from friction and give structural integrity to the tissue. The perimysium (surrounding the fascicles) may also be involved in transmitting contractile movements across the muscle.

4. The all-or-none response refers to the way in which an individual muscle fiber contracts maximally (if the stimulus is

strong enough) or not at all (if it is not).

5. Without dystrophin there is no structural link between the muscle fibers and the extracellular matrix. Calcium penetrates the plasma membrane (sarcolemma) of the muscle cells and damages them, eventually destroying the muscle cells (fibers).

The Sliding Filament Theory (page 73)

1. (a) **Myosin**: Has a moveable head that provides a power stroke when activated.
    (b) **Actin**: Two protein molecules twisted in a double helix shape that form the thin filament of a myofibril.
    (c) **Calcium ions**: Bind to the blocking molecules, causing them to move and expose the myosin binding site.
    (d) **Troponin-tropomyosin**: Bind to actin molecule in a way that prevents myosin head from forming a cross bridge.
    (e) **ATP**: Supplies energy for flexing of the myosin head (power stroke).

2. (a) By changing the frequency of stimulation, so that fibers receive impulses at a greater rate (frequency summation).
    (b) By changing the number and size of motor units recruited (a few motor units = a small contraction, maximum number of motor units = maximum contraction).

3. (a) Calcium ions and ATP.
    (b) Calcium ions are released from a store in the sarcoplasmic reticulum when an action potential arrives. ATP is present in the muscle fiber and is hydrolyzed by ATPase enzymes on the myosin.

Muscle Tone and Posture (page 74)

1. (a) Muscle tone is the continuous and passive partial contraction of muscles giving a firm appearance.
    (b) At any one time, a few fibers in a muscle are always contracting involuntarily (different fibers at different times).

2. (a) The **muscle spindle organ** monitors the degree of stretch (contraction) in a muscle and provides information to bring about adjustment of contraction.
    (b) **Intrafusal fibers parallel to extrafusal fibers**: When the muscle relaxes, it lengthens and the muscle spindle is stretched. The stretching results in a reflex adjustment of contraction (usually to maintain tone).
    Sensory neurons in non-contractile region: When non-contractile portion is stretched (it cannot, itself, adjust its length), sensory neurons are stimulated.
    Motor neuron synapses: When the motor impulses arrive to adjust state of contraction, both the extrafusal and intrafusal fibers are adjusted appropriately.

The Mechanics of Movement (page 75)

1. (a) Prime mover: the muscle primarily responsible for the movement.
    (b) Antagonist: the muscle that opposes the prime mover. i.e. relaxes when prime mover contracts. Its action can be protective in preventing over-stretching of the prime mover during contraction.
    (c) Synergist: assists the prime mover by fine-tuning the direction of limb movement.

2. Muscles can only contract and relax, therefore they can only pull on a bone; they cannot push it. To produce movement, two muscles must act as **antagonistic** pairs to move a bone to and from different positions.

3. Muscles have an origin on one (less moveable) bone and an insertion on another (more moveable) bone. When the muscle contracts across the joint connecting the two bones, the insertion moves towards the origin, therefore moving the limb. To raise a limb, the flexor (prime mover in this case) contracts pulling the limb bone up (extensor/antagonist relaxed). To lower the limb, the extensor contracts, pulling the limb down (flexor relaxed).

4. Bones are rigid and movement occurs only at joints. The degree of movement allowed depends the type of joint. The

© 2009-2013 **BIOZONE** International
ISBN: 978-1-927173-59-6
Photocopying Prohibited

bones of the limbs, which need to be freely moveable are connected by synovial joints. Body parts where movement is not desirable, such as the joints of the skull, are largely rigid.

5. (a) Radius (radial tuberosity)
   (b) Ulna
   (c) Triceps
   (d) Rotation of ulna and radius

6. (a) Elbow extension
   (b) Triceps

7. (a) Nodding head = flexion and extension
   (b) Hitching a ride = abduction

Energy for Muscle Contraction (page 77)

1. Lactic acid quickly builds up as a waste product of the glycolytic pathway. Lactic acid inhibits glycogen breakdown and impedes muscular contraction, so the time period for its use is limited.

2. **Energy systems:**
   ATP-CP
   ATP supplied by: Breakdown of CP
   Duration of ATP supply: Short (3-15 s)
   Glycolytic
   ATP supplied by: Anaerobic breakdown of glycogen
   Duration of ATP supply: A few minutes at most.
   Oxidative
   ATP supplied by: Complete aerobic (oxidative) breakdown of glycogen to CO_2 and water.
   Duration of ATP supply: Prolonged but dependent on ability to supply oxygen to the muscles (fitness).

3. (a) Region **A**: Oxygen deficit: the amount of oxygen needed for aerobic supply but not supplied by breathing, i.e. an oxygen deficit builds up.
   (b) Region **B**: Oxygen debt: the extra oxygen required (taken in) despite the drop in energy demand. The debt is used to replace oxygen reserves, restore CP, and break down lactic acid.
   Note: Both components (deficit and debt) are often used synonymously (as oxygen debt) although they are not quite the same. The deficit is the oxygen shortfall incurred during exercise; the debt is the amount of oxygen required to restore oxygen and energy stores to resting levels. Their values are not necessarily the same.

4. Oxygen uptake does not immediately return to resting levels because of the extra oxygen required to restore oxygen and energy levels (the oxygen debt).

5. Oxygen supply is increased by increased rate and depth of breathing (increasing gas exchange rate) and increased blood flow (increased gas transport).

6. Lactic acid levels in the blood rise for a time after exercise because the lactic acid is transported in the blood from the muscles (where it has accumulated) to the liver, where it is metabolized to CO_2 and water.

Muscle Fatigue (page 79)

1. Lactic acid accumulation in muscle tissue results in lowered pH and inhibition of cellular activity.

2. (a) Fall in ATP production
   (b) Fall in calcium release

3. In a long distance race, such as a marathon, ATP continues to be produced **aerobically** until all energy supplies are exhausted. In a sprint ATP is produced **anaerobically** until the oxygen debt has been repaid.

Muscle Physiology and Performance (page 80)

1. (a)-(c) Any three, in any order. Endurance training improves the oxidative function of muscle through:
   – Improved oxidation of glycogen, which increases the capacity of the muscle to generate ATP aerobically.

– Increased capacity of the muscle to oxidize fats, which allows glycogen to be used at a slower rate.
– Increased myoglobin content in the muscle, which stores oxygen and aids oxygen delivery to mitochondria.
– An increase in the number of capillaries surrounding muscle fibers increases oxygen delivery and removal of wastes.
– An increase in the size and density of mitochondria in the muscle.
– An increase in the concentration and activity of Krebs cycle enzymes improves capacity for aerobic respiration.
– An increase in fiber size which can accommodate an increase in mitochondria, myoglobin, and glycogen storage.

2. **Fast twitch** fibers are large, pale fibers with rapid contraction rates, rapid rates of ATP production, and high power generation. They work anaerobically, but fatigue quickly, and these properties suit them to short bursts of activity where maximal force is required quickly (as in sprinting or power lifting). **Slow twitch** fibers, in contrast, are darker (red) due to the presence of large amounts of myoglobin, they are small in diameter and have a slower rate of ATP production and a slower contraction rate. They work aerobically, but fatigue slowly, so they are suited to activities where endurance and prolonged activity at a sustainable level is required. **Note**: Fast twitch fibers will be (preferentially) developed and recruited in sprint trained athletes. Slow twitch fibers will be (preferentially) developed and recruited in endurance trained athletes. Muscle contains a mix of fiber types, providing the capacity for both explosive effort and endurance.

KEY TERMS: Mix and Match (page 81)

actin (thin filament) (K), antagonistic pair (C), blood lactate (I), cardiac muscle (T), cross bridge (S), fast twitch (U), filament (=myofilament) (H), muscle fatigue (E), muscle fiber (A), myofibril (L), myosin (thick filament) (G), neuromuscular junction (O), oxygen debt (J), prime mover (B), sarcomere (M), sarcoplasmic reticulum (N), skeletal (=striated) muscle (V), sliding filament hypothesis (Q), slow twitch (D), smooth muscle (R), tropomyosin (F), troponin (P).

Nervous Regulatory Systems (page 85)

1. (a) The **sensory receptors** receive sensory information (information about the environment) and respond by generating an electrical response (message).
   (b) The **central nervous system** (CNS) processes the sensory input and coordinates an appropriate response (through motor output).
   (c) A system of **effectors** bring about an appropriate response.

2. (a) and (b) any two in any order:
   • Nervous control involves transmission across synapses, hormonal control involves transport of chemicals in the blood.
   • Nervous control is rapid, hormonal control is slower.
   • Nervous control acts in the short term and its effects are short lived, hormonal control is longer acting.
   • Nervous control is direct and through specific pathways, hormonal control is widespread, affecting target cells throughout the body (although these may be quite specific).
   • Nervous control causes muscular action directly, hormonal control generally acts by changing metabolic activity.

The Nervous System (page 86)

1. (a) Sensory: Reception of internal and external stimuli.
   (b) Integrative: Interpretation of sensory messages.
   (c) Motor: Initiation and coordination of an appropriate response to the sensory input.

2. (a) **CNS**: Brain and spinal cord. The brain has ultimate control of almost all body activities (except simple spinal reflexes). The spinal cord interprets simple reflexes and relays impulses to and from the brain.
   (b) **PNS**: All nerves and sensory receptors outside the CNS. Divided into sensory and motor divisions. The motor division controls both voluntary (somatic) and involuntary (autonomic) responses. Regulates sensory reception,

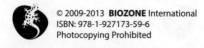

© 2009-2013 **BIOZONE** International
ISBN: 978-1-927173-59-6
Photocopying Prohibited

relays impulses to the CNS, brings about the motor response.

3. Separation of the motor division of the PNS into somatic and autonomic divisions allows essential functions to occur without conscious involvement. In this way, the conscious part of the brain is not overwhelmed by having to coordinate every motor response. This improves efficiency of motor function.

The Autonomic Nervous System (page 87)

1. (a) **Sympathetic** NS: Fibers originate from the spinal cord in thoracic and lumbar regions. Preganglionic fibers are short and release acetylcholine. Post-ganglionic fibers are long and usually release norepinephrine. The sympathetic NS is active when the body is preparing for fight or flight.
   (b) **Parasympathetic** NS: Fibers originate from the brainstem and the sacral region of the spinal cord. Preganglionic fibers are long and postganglionic fibers are very short. All parasympathetic fibers are cholinergic and release acetylcholine. The parasympathetic NS is more active in conserving energy and replenishing energy reserves ('feed or breed' or 'rest and digest').

2. (a) The sympathetic division of the ANS is more active when the body is preparing for action ('fight or flight') while the parasympathetic division is more active in conserving energy and replenishing energy reserves ('feed or breed' or 'rest and digest'). In general, the sympathetic NS stimulates where the parasympathetic inhibits and vice versa.
   (b) Most sympathetic postganglionic nerves release norepinephrine which enters the bloodstream and is deactivated slowly. In contrast, parasympathetic nerves release acetylcholine which is rapidly deactivated at the synapse with short-lived localized effects.

3. Autonomic nervous system controls visceral motor functions through reflex activity. Any of the following:
   Pupil reflex:
   Cranial reflex to light. Stimulation of the eye by bright light causes reflex constriction of the pupil mediated through the parasympathetic nervous system.
   Control of heart rate:
   Increase in arterial pressure causes reflex stimulation of the cardioinhibitory centre through the parasympathetic division, slowing heart rate and decreasing arterial BP to normal. If BP falls, reflex acceleration of the heart takes place: the baroreceptors do not stimulate the cardioinhibitory centre, and the accelerator centre (sympathetic) is free to dominate. A similar reflex (the Bainbridge or right heart reflex) operates in response to increased venous return. Increased return of blood to the heart causes reflex stimulation of the accelerator centre, causing heart rate to increase (sympathetic).
   Control of digestive secretions and gut motility:
   Parasympathetic stimulation increases peristalsis (gut motility), promotes insulin and enzyme secretion and sugar storage. This readies the body for rest. Sympathetic stimulation prepares the body for action by decreasing peristalsis, inhibiting insulin and enzyme secretion and releasing sugar into the bloodstream. Note: The enteric nervous system (ENS) is an independent part of the ANS, comprising of special neurones. These neurones are located in specialised bundles in the gut wall and they provide localised reflexes during the digestion of food.

4. Bladder emptying is under reflex control and is stimulated by stretching of the bladder wall. Stretching causes both a conscious desire to urinate and an unconscious reflex contraction of the bladder wall and relaxation of the internal urethral sphincter. The conscious part of the brain also sends impulses to relax the external urethral sphincter. Because both conscious and unconscious controls are involved, urination can be voluntarily stopped and started at will (**recognition** of and response to the cues for bladder emptying develop around two years of age).

5. A sudden decrease in blood pressure would result in the sympathetic NS increasing the constriction of the coronary blood vessels and subsequent increase in the rate and force of contraction of the heart. As a result, blood pressure would rise.

6. Note: Noradrenaline = norepinephrine.
   Inhalation of the drug results in dilation of the bronchioles (airways) in the lungs and the patient is able to breath more easily.

The Human Brain (page 89)

1. (a) Breathing/heartbeat: brainstem (medulla)
   (b) Memory/emotion: cerebrum
   (c) Posture/balance: cerebellum
   (d) Autonomic functions: hypothalamus
   (e) Visual processing: occipital lobe
   (f) Body temperature: hypothalamus
   (g) Language: motor and sensory speech areas
   (h) Muscular movement: primary motor area

2. The brain is protected against physical damage and infection by the bony skull, by the meninges overlying the delicate brain tissue, and by the fluid-filled ventricles, which absorb shocks and deliver nutritive substances (via cerebrospinal fluid) to the brain tissue. The blood-brain barrier formed by the endothelial tight junctions of capillaries surrounding the brain is also the main protection against toxins and infection as microbes and many large molecules cannot cross it.

3. (a) The CSF is produced by the choroid plexuses, which are the capillary clusters on the roof of each ventricle. It circulates through the ventricles and returns to the blood via projections of the arachnoid membrane.
   (b) If this return flow is blocked, fluid builds up in the ventricles causing hydrocephalus, and consequently pressure on the brain tissue and brain damage.

Neuron Structure (page 91)

1. (a) Any one of:
   • Motor neurons have many short dendrites and a single (usually long) axon.
   • In sensory neurons, the cell body gives rise to two axonal branches (one central, one peripheral). The axons are usually short.
   • A sensory neuron has a sense organ at the 'receptor' end or it synapses with a sense organ (as in the retina of the eye). In a motor neuron the dendrites receive their stimuli from other neurons.
   (b) Any one of:
   • Motor neuron transmits impulses from CNS to muscles or glands (effectors).
   • Sensory neuron transmits impulses from sensory receptors to the CNS.

2. (a) Any one of:
   • Motor neurons have a long axon.
   • Relay neurons have a short axon within the CNS.
   (b) Any one of:
   • Motor neuron transmits impulses from CNS to muscles or glands (effectors).
   • Relay neuron transmits impulses from sensory neurons to motor neurons within the CNS.

3. Relay neurons lie within the CNS, so impulses are not transmitted far. The axons of motor neurons extend to effectors in the peripheral NS so their axons are often very long (extending to the periphery of the body).

4. Muscles and glands.

5. (a) Myelination increases the speed of impulse conduction.
   (b) Oligodendrocytes
   (c) Schwann cells
   (d) Neurons in the PNS frequently have to transmit over long distances so speed of impulse conduction is critical to efficient function.

6. (a) Myelination prevents ions from entering or leaving the axon and so stops leakage of charge across the neuron membrane. The current is carried in the cytoplasm so that the action potential at one node (gap in the sheath) is sufficient to trigger an action potential at the next. Myelin also reduces energy expenditure since fewer ions overall need to be pumped to restore resting potential after an action potential has passed.

© 2009-2013 **BIOZONE** International
ISBN: 978-1-927173-59-6
Photocopying Prohibited

(b) Faster conduction speeds enable more rapid responses to stimuli.

7. The destruction of the myelin prevents those (previously myelinated) axons from conducting. Without insulation, the neuron membrane leaks ions and the local current is attenuated and insufficient to depolarize the next node. **Note**: myelinated axons only have gated channels at their nodes, so action potentials can only be generated at node regions in those axons that were previously myelinated.

Neuroglia (page 93)

1. Neuroglia are the cells that support and protect neurons. They hold them in place, insulate them, and supply them with nutrients and oxygen.

2. (a) Astrocytes are supportive cells anchoring neurons to capillaries and supporting the blood-brain barrier. They also help repair brain tissue after injury. They have many processes to connect the neurons and capillaries.
   (b) Ependymal cells line the ventricles of the brain and the central canal of the spinal cord and circulate and absorb the CSF. They have cilia and microvilli to facilitate this.
   (c) Microglia have a role in defense of the central nervous tissue. Phagocytic so they can recognize and engulf foreign material.
   (d) Oligodenrocytes produce insulating myelin sheaths around the axons of neurons in the CNS. They are highly extensible and can wrap around up to 50 axons.

Reflexes (page 94)

1. Higher reasoning is not a preferable feature of reflexes because it would slow down the response time. The adaptive value of reflexes is in allowing a very rapid response to a stimulus.

2. A spinal reflex involves integration within the spinal cord, e.g. knee jerk (monosynaptic) or pain withdrawal (polysynaptic). A cranial reflex involves integration within the brain stem (e.g. pupil reflex).

3. (a) A monosynaptic reflex arc involves just two neurones and one synapse (e.g. knee jerk reflex) and a polysynaptic reflex arc involves two synapses through a relay or interneurone, e.g. pain withdrawal.
   (b) A monosynaptic reflex arc, because there is one less synapse over which diffusion of neurotransmitter must occur.

4. (a) Newborn reflexes equip them with the appropriate survival behaviour in their otherwise helpless state: the rooting reflex helps them to locate a nipple, the suckling reflex insures feeding, the startle reflex induces crying, invoking a parental care response, the grasp reflex ensures they keep contact with (usually) the mother.
   (b) The presence of these reflexes indicates appropriate development. An absence of reflex behaviours in newborns may indicate neural damage or developmental impairment.

The Nerve Impulse (page 95)

1. An action potential is a self-regenerating depolarization (electrochemical signal) that allows excitable cells (such as muscle and nerve cells) to carry a signal over a (varying) distance.

2. (a) Neurons are able to transmit electrical impulses.
   (b) Supporting cells are not able to transmit impulses.
3. (a) Depolarization: Na+ channels open and Na+ ions flood into the cell.
   (b) Repolarisation: Na+ channels close, K+ channels open and K+ ions move out of the cell.

4. (1) When the neuron receives the threshold-level stimulus, the membrane briefly becomes more permeability to Na$^+$, which floods into the cell (through voltage gated channels), resulting in a depolarization. (2)　After the Na$^+$ influx, the Na$^+$ gates close and K$^+$ gates open, causing a brief hyperpolarization before the resting potential is restored. (3) The hyperpolarization means that for a short time (1-2 ms) the neuron cannot respond, so the impulse only travels in one direction (away from the stimulus).

5. Resting potential is restored by closure of the Na$^+$ channels and opening of the K$^+$ channels. K$^+$ moves out to restore the negative charge to the cell interior. All voltage activated gates close and the resting state is restored.

6. (a) Action potential travels by saltatory conduction, with depolarization and action potential generation at the modes of Ranvier..
   (b) Action potential spreads by local current (conduction is slower).

7. Because the refractory period makes the neuron unable to respond for a brief period after an action potential has passed, the impulse can pass in only one direction along the nerve (away from the cell body).

Neurotransmitters (page 97)

1. To transmit signals from one neuron to the next across the synapse.

2. (a) Electricity changes the rate of neuron depolarization and changes the amount of neurotransmitter released.
   (b) The neurotransmitter took time to move through the solution from one heart to the next, causing the delay.

3. Neurotransmitters (NT) can be excitatory or inhibitory depending on the properties of the post-synaptic membrane/receptors. Binding of a particular NT may produce an excitatory response in some post-synaptic cells and an inhibitory response in others.

Chemical Synapses (page 98)

1. A **synapse** is a junction between the end of one axon and the dendrite or cell body of a receiving neuron. **Note**: A synapse can also occur between the end of one axon and a muscle cell (neuromuscular junction).

2. Arrival of a nerve impulse at the end of the axon causes an influx of calcium. This induces the vesicles to release their neurotransmitter into the cleft.

3. Delay at the synapse is caused by the time it takes for the neurotransmitter to diffuse across the gap (synaptic cleft) between neurons.

4. (a) Neurotransmitter (NT) is degraded into component molecules by enzyme activity on the membrane of the receiving neuron.
   (b) The neurotransmitter must be deactivated so that it does not continue to stimulate the receiving neuron (continued stimulation would lead to depletion of neurotransmitter and fatigue of the nerve). Deactivation allows recovery of the neuron so that it can respond to further impulses.
   (c) Transmission is unidirectional because the synapse is asymmetric in structure and function. The presynaptic membrane does not possess the receptors for the NT and the postsynaptic neuron does not have the stores of NT within vesicles.

5. **The amount of neurotransmitter released** influences the response of the receiving cell (response strength is proportional to amount of neurotransmitter released).

Integration at Synapses (page 99)

1. Integration refers to the interpretation and coordination (by the central nervous system) of inputs from many sources (inputs may be inhibitory or excitatory).

2. (a) **Summation**: The additive effect of presynaptic inputs (impulses) in the postsynaptic cell (neuron or muscle fiber).
   (b) **Spatial summation** refers to the summation of impulses from **separate** axon terminals arriving simultaneously at the postsynaptic cell. **Temporal summation** refers to the arrival of several impulses from a **single** axon terminal in rapid succession (the postsynaptic potentials are so close together in time that they can sum to generate an action potential).

© 2009-2013 **BIOZONE** International
ISBN: 978-1-927173-59-6
Photocopying Prohibited

3. (a) **Acetylcholine** is the NT involved; arrival of an action potential at the neuromuscular junction causes the release of Ach from the synaptic knobs.
   (b) Ach causes **depolarization** of the postsynaptic membrane (in this case, the sarcolemma). **Note**: The depolarization in response to the arrival of an action potential at the postsynaptic cell is essentially the same as that occurring at any excitatory synapse involving Ach neurotransmitter.

Drugs at Synapses (page 100)

1. (a) and (b) any of in any order:
   - Drug can act as a direct agonist, binding to and activating Ach receptors on the postsynaptic membrane, e.g. nicotine.
   - Drug can act as an indirect agonist, preventing the breakdown of Ach, thereby causing continued response in the postsynaptic cell, e.g. therapeutic drugs used to treat Alzheimer's disease.
   - Drug can act as an antagonist, competing for Ach binding sites and reducing or blocking the response of the postsynaptic cell, e.g. atropine or curare.

2. Atropine and curare are direct antagonists because they compete for the same binding sites (as Ach) on the postsynaptic membrane (hence **direct**) and block sodium influx so that impulses are not generated (hence **antagonist** = against the usual action).

3. Curare is used to cause flaccid paralysis (relaxed or without tone) to the isolated abdominal region in order to facilitate operative procedure (of course, the drug is administered as a carefully produced formulation).

Chemical Imbalances in the Brain (page 101)

1. Neurotransmitters are chemicals that transfer signals between neurons across a synapse (synaptic cleft). A neurotransmitter is released from the presynaptic neuron into the synaptic cleft where it interacts with a postsynaptic neuron to cause a response. The amount of neurotransmitter released influences the response of the receiving cell.

2. (a) Parkinson's disease is caused by a reduction in dopamine production due to the loss of nerve cells in the substantia nigra region of the brain. This reduces the stimulation in the motor cortex and results in slow physical movement and uncontrollable tremors.
   (b) Depression is caused by reduced serotonin released from the raphe nuclei resulting in reduced stimulation of neurons in the brain, but especially those related to emotion. People with depression often have feelings of low self esteem, guilt, regret, and suffer physical tiredness.

Detecting Changing States (page 102)

1. **Stimulus**: Any physical or chemical change in the environment capable of provoking a response in an organism.

2. Communication systems (here referring to the means by which changes in the environment are communicated to effectors) are necessary in order to respond appropriately to environmental stimuli. Appropriate responses aid survival and enable effective interpretation about the changing state of the environment. For example, pain withdrawal response prevents a burned hand, running away from a snarling dog avoids attack etc.

3. (a) Any from the examples provided (or others). Answers provided as stimulus (receptor):
   Blood pH/carbon dioxide level (chemoreceptors in blood vessels); blood pressure (baroreceptors); stretch (proprioreceptors, e.g. muscle spindle).
   (b) Chemoreceptors maintain breathing and heart rates, baroreceptors maintain blood pressure, proprioreceptors maintain movement, photoreceptors maintain vision.

The Basis of Sensory Perception (page 103)

1. Sensory receptors convert stimulus energy (e.g. electromagnetic radiation) into electrochemical energy (a change in membrane potential).

2. All receptors receive and respond to stimuli by producing receptor potentials.

3. The stimulus energy opens an ion channel in the membrane leading to ion flux and a localized change in membrane potential, e.g. an influx of Na^+ and a depolarization. This localized change in membrane potential is called a receptor potential and it may lead directly or indirectly to an action potential.

4. (a) Receptor potentials are localized depolarizations. They are graded (of different sub-threshold magnitude) and not self-propagating.
   (b) Receptor potentials can sum together and increase in amplitude to reach threshold for generation of an action potential. When the stimulus is very strong, receptor potentials are larger (remember they are graded potentials), threshold is reached more rapidly, and action potential frequency is higher.

Encoding Information (page 104)

1. (a) Stimulus strength is encoded by the frequency of action potentials.
   (b) Frequency modulation is the only way to convey information about the stimulus strength to the brain because action potentials are 'all or none' (information can not be communicated by variations in amplitude).

2. In the Pacinian corpuscle, stronger pressure produces larger receptor potentials, threshold is reached more rapidly, and action potential frequency is higher.

3. Sensory adaptation allows the nervous system to cease responding to constant stimuli that do not change in intensity. Constant, background sensory information can be ignored.

The Structure of the Eye (page 105)

1. (a) **Cornea**: Responsible for most of the refraction (bending) of the incoming light.
   (b) **Ciliary body**: Secretes the aqueous humour which helps to maintain the shape of the eye and assists in refraction.
   (c) **Iris**: Regulates the amount of light entering the eye for vision in bright and dim light.

2. (a) The incoming light is refracted (primarily by the cornea) and the amount entering the eye is regulated by constriction of the pupil. The degree of refraction is adjusted through **accommodation** (changes to the shape of the lens) so that a sharp image is formed on the retina.
   (b) Accommodation is achieved by the action of the ciliary muscles pulling on the elastic lens and changing its shape. **Note**: When the ciliary muscle contracts there is decreased pressure on the suspensory ligament and the lens becomes more convex (to focus on near objects). When the ciliary muscle relaxes there is increased tension on the suspensory ligament and the lens is pulled into a thinner shape (to focus on distant objects).

3. (a) The pupil is the hole through which light enters the eye. By constricting (in bright light), the pupil can narrow the diameter of this entry point and prevent light rays entering from the periphery. In dim light, the opposite happens; the pupil expands to allow more light into the eye.
   (b) Control of over the entry of light is appropriate as a reflex activity because the response is immediate and unconscious. In this way, the eye can be protected against damage and vision optimized without the need to consider the action necessary (which would be slow and inefficient).

4. (a) Point of focus would be in front of the retina.
   (b) Point of focus would be behind the retina (image on the retina is blurred).

© 2009-2013 **BIOZONE** International
ISBN: 978-1-927173-59-6
Photocopying Prohibited

5. (a) **Myopia:** Concave lens diverges the incoming light rays so that they have to travel further through the eyeball and are focused directly on the retina.
   (b) **Hypermetropia:** Convex lens converges incoming light so that the image falls directly on the retina.

The Physiology of Vision (page 107)

1. (a) The retina is the region of the eye responsible for receiving and responding to light. It contains the pigment-containing photoreceptor cells (the rods and cones) which absorb the light and produce an electrical response. This response is converted by other cells in the retina into action potentials in the optic nerve.
   (b) The optic nerve is formed from the axons of the retinal ganglion cells, and carries the action potentials from the retina through the optic chiasma to the visual cortex in the cerebrum.
   (c) The central fovea is the region of the retina with the highest cone density where acuity is greatest (sharpest vision).

2.

Feature	Rod cells	Cone cells
Visual pigment(s):	Rhodopsin (no color vision)	Iodopsin (three types)
Visual acuity:	Low	High
Overall function:	Vision in dim light, high sensitivity	Color vision, vision in bright light

3. (a)-(c) in any order
   (a) **Photoreceptor cells (rods and cones)** respond to light by producing graded receptor potentials.
   (b) **Bipolar neurons** form synapses with the rods and cones and transmit the changes in membrane potential to the ganglion cells. Each cone synapses with one bipolar (=high acuity) whereas many rods synapse with one bipolar cell (=high sensitivity).
   (c) **Ganglion cells** synapse with the bipolar cells and respond with depolarization and generation of action potentials. Their axons form the optic nerve.

4. (a) **Horizontal cells** are interconnecting neurons that help to integrate and regulate the input from multiple photoreceptor cells. They enhance information about contrast.
   (b) **Amacrine cells** form synapses with bipolar cells and work laterally to affect output from the bipolar cells, enhancing information about light level.

5. Several rod cells synapse with each bipolar cell. This gives poor acuity but high sensitivity. Each cone cell synapses with only one bipolar cell and this gives high acuity but poor sensitivity.

6. (a) A photochemical pigment is a molecule (e.g. contained in the membranes of the photoreceptor cells) that undergoes a structural change when exposed to light (and is therefore light-sensitive).
   (b) Rhodopsin in rods and iodopsin in cones.

7. Light falling on the retina causes structural changes in the photopigments of the rods and cones. These changes lead to the development of graded electrical signals (hyperpolarizations) which spread from the rods and cones, via the bipolar neurons, to the ganglion cells. The ganglion cells respond by depolarization and transmit action potentials to the brain.

Skin Senses (page 109)

Exemplar results for two point threshold test (in mm). Results will vary between individuals and trials, but the general trend of the data should be:

Forearm:	26 mm
Back of hand:	9 mm
Palm of hand:	7 mm
Fingertip:	1-2 mm
Lips:	< 1 mm

1. Lips and/or fingertips.

2. Forearm.

3. The lips and/or fingertips need to be sensitive to carry out their functions (locating and tasting food, communication etc,). They therefore need to have a great number of receptors. The forearm requires many fewer as it is not involved in intricate tasks.

Hearing (page 110)

1. (a) **Ear drum:** Vibrates in response to sound waves.
   (b) **Ear ossicles:** Transmit the sound waves from the ear drum to the smaller oval window.
   (c) **Oval window:** Amplifies the sound waves before they enter the fluid filled inner ear (because of its smaller surface area).
   (d) **Sensory hair cells:** Respond to the stimulus of pressure waves in the fluid filled inner ear by generating electrical impulses.
   (e) **Auditory nerve:** Transmits the impulses from the sensory hair cells to the brain for processing.

2. Sound waves are converted into pressure waves in the fluid. Because fluid is non-compressible, the pressure wave moves the membranes in the cochlea, causing the hair cells to be stimulated.

Taste and Smell (page 111)

1. Chemical sense relies on the chemicals (scent molecules) binding to membrane-bound sensory receptors and causing a change in membrane potential in the sensory cell (signal transduction). These electrochemical messages are relayed to the appropriate centers in the brain where they are interpreted.

2. Example only:
   10 s: 1 (very strong)
   20 s: 2 (quite strong)
   30 s: 3 (noticeable)
   40 s: 4 (weak)
   50 s: 5 (very faint)
   60 s: 6 (could not detect)

3. (a) The sense of smell (to that scent) declines.
   (b) Sensory adaptation. The sensory cells adapt to the stimulus and cease responding to it.
   (c) It is adaptive to stop responding to unchanging stimuli. Appropriate responses are directed to new stimuli.

Aging and the Nervous System (page 112)

1. (a) There is a cumulative loss of neurons with age from about age 30 and these losses affect cognitive function.
   (b) Cognitive decline can be slowed with good diet (including reduced alcohol intake), and mental and physical exercise.

Alzheimer's and the Brain (page 113)

1. Alzheimer's results when neurons, and their connections, are lost at an accelerated rate in the brain. Loss of processing ability affects a number of functions including memory, reasoning and language.

2. A mutation for the APP gene has been discovered within families who demonstrate a history of Alzheimer's. The protein is thought to be involved in synapse formation and neural plasticity.

3. Alzheimer's sufferers suffer an **accelerated** loss of neurons and show reduced brain activity, particularly in regions that are important for memory and intellectual processing, such as the cerebral cortex and hippocampus. **Note:** The most recent evidence indicates that, during normal aging, there is a loss of synaptic function in the brain, but the neurons themselves are not lost. In Alzheimer's, there is a pathological loss of the neurons themselves.

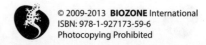 © 2009-2013 **BIOZONE** International
ISBN: 978-1-927173-59-6
Photocopying Prohibited

KEY TERMS: Mix and Match (page 114)

action potential (I), autonomic nervous system (M), axon (K), biological transducer (B), brain (T), central nervous system (H), cerebellum (F), cerebrum (Y), chemoreception (U), dendrites (AA), depolarization (Q), glial cells (O), integration (Z), motor neuron (X), myelinated nerve (V), nervous system (A), neuron (J), nodes of Ranvier (P), peripheral nervous system (W), saltatory conduction (E), Schwann cells (L), sense organ (S), sensory receptor (R), somatic nervous system (D), spinal cord (C), stimulus (G), synapse (N).

Cell Signalling (page 116)

1. (a) **Endocrine signalling**, where a hormone is carried in the blood between the endocrine gland/organ where it is produced to target cells.
   (b) **Paracrine signalling**, where cell signalling molecules are released to act on target cells in the immediate vicinity, e.g. at synapses or between cells during development.
   (c) **Autocrine signalling**, where cells produce and react to their own signals (e.g. growth factors from T cells stimulate the production of more T cells).

2. The three signalling types all have in common some kind of chemical messenger or signal molecule (ligand) and a receptor molecule (on the target cells, which may or may not be on the cell producing the signal).

Signal Transduction (page 117)

1. If the membrane receptor is an alpha type, epinephrine acts through G protein activation and the G protein directly alters cell function. If the membrane receptor is a beta type, epinephrine acts through cyclic AMP as a second messenger. Cyclic AMP activates a signal cascade that brings about the cellular response.

2. A signal is amplified by a signal transduction cascade. At each step of the cascade many molecules are activated, amplifying the original signal, and causing vast numbers of molecules to be activated or changed in some way. The activation of so many molecules causes a cellular response.

3. Both involve a specific interaction between one molecule and its specific receptor region. In the case of a hormone, the hormone binds to its specific membrane receptor. In an enzyme-substrate reaction, the substrate interacts with the active site of the enzyme.

Hormonal Regulation (page 118)

1. (a) **Antagonistic hormones**: Two hormones that have contrasting (counteracting) effects on metabolism. Examples: insulin and glucagon, parathormone (increases blood calcium) and calcitonin (lowers blood calcium).
   (b) In general principle, the product of a series of (hormone controlled) reactions controls its own production by turning off the pathway when it reaches a certain level. If there is too little of the product, its production is switched on again.

2. Only the target cells have the appropriate receptors on the membrane to respond to the hormone. Other (nontarget) cells will not be affected.

3. (a) Hormones must circulate in the blood to reach the target cells and a metabolic response must be initiated. This takes some time.
   (b) Hormones bring about a metabolic change and often start a sequence of cascading, interrelated events. Once started, these events take time to conclude. Nervous responses continue only for the time that the stimulation continues.

The Endocrine System (page 119)

1. A **neurotransmitter** is a chemical messenger that is released at a chemical synapse and stimulates a post-synaptic cell. In contrast, **hormones** are chemical messengers that are released from specialized cells into the blood where they circulate and stimulate target cells. **Note**: Some hormones (e.g. epinephrine) may also function as neurotransmitters when they occur at synapses.

2. (a) Pituitary gland - master gland secreting at least nine hormones.....
   (b) Ovaries - produce estrogen and progesterone in response to hormones from the pituitary
   (c) Pineal gland - Secretes melatonin to regulate sleep patterns....
   (d) Parathyroid glands - the hormone from this gland regulates the levels of calcium in the blood.
   (e) Thyroid - produces hormones involved in the regulation of metabolic rate.

3. Any number of examples are possible. Typical examples include:
   (a) **Hormonal stimulus**: Adrenocorticotropic hormone (ACTH) from the anterior pituitary stimulates the production and secretion of androgens and cortisol from the adrenal cortex.
   (b) **Humoral stimulus**: High blood glucose stimulates release of insulin from the endocrine tissue of the pancreas. Low blood glucose levels stimulate release of glucagon.
   (c) **Neural stimulus**: Sympathetic nervous stimulation of the adrenal medulla causes the release of norepinephrine (noradrenaline).

4. Several examples are described. In general, blood hormone level provides the information (via negative feedback) to increase or decrease secretion. For anterior pituitary hormones, this is mediated via hypothalamic releasing factors.
   (a) Target tissue: thyroid gland.
       Controlling hormone: TSH from anterior pituitary.
   (b) Homeostatic function: TSH promotes the release of thyroid hormones from the thyroid gland. These hormones are primarily responsible for regulating metabolism.
   (c) Regulation: TSH is regulated by TRH from the hypothalamus. TRH stimulates the anterior pituitary to produce TSH. The release of TSH from the pituitary is regulated by the level of thyroid hormones in the blood through negative feedback. When thyroid hormone levels in the blood are low, this is registered by the hypothalamus and TSH secretion is increased. Conversely, when thyroid hormone levels in the blood are high, TSH secretion is reduced.

   (a) Target tissue: Mammary glands.
       Controlling hormone: Prolactin (secreted by the anterior pituitary).
   (b) Homeostatic function: Stimulates and maintains milk production and secretion.
   (c) Regulation: Via releasing (PRH) and inhibiting (PIH) hormones from the hypothalamus.

   (a) Target tissue: Most tissues, especially skeletal.
       Controlling hormone: Growth hormone (GH) (secreted by the anterior pituitary).
   (b) Homeostatic function: Stimulates protein metabolism and general growth of body cells, especially bone.
   (c) Regulation: Via releasing and inhibiting hormones from the hypothalamus. When GH levels are low, release is stimulated by growth hormone releasing hormone. When GH levels are high, release is inhibited by growth hormone inhibiting hormone.

   (a) Target tissue: Liver, blood vessels, kidneys.
       Controlling hormone: Epinephrine (secreted by the adrenal glands).
   (b) Homeostatic function: Increases blood sugar, constricts blood vessels in kidney and liver. Prepares for fight or flight.
   (c) Regulation: Nervous stimulation of the adrenal glands via the hypothalamus stimulates increased secretion of adrenaline. Low blood sugar also stimulates adrenaline secretion directly.

   (a) Target tissue: Kidney.
       Controlling hormone: Antidiuretic hormone (ADH) (secreted by the posterior pituitary).
   (b) Homeostatic function: Promotes reabsorption of water

18

and decreases urine volume.

(c) Regulation: Secretion stimulated by low blood volume (water concentration), pain, stress, anxiety, nicotine. Alcohol inhibits ADH secretion.

5. (a) The adrenal gland has two functionally and structurally distinct regions, and outer cortex and an inner medulla.

(b) The medulla secretes epinephrine and norepinephrine into the blood in response to direct sympathetic nervous system stimulation. The adrenal cortex secretes steroid hormones (corticosteroids and androgens). Its secretion is regulated by neuroendocrine hormones secreted from the pituitary gland and by the renin-angiotensin system.

(c) The pituitary is responsible for regulating (through ACTH) the secretion of hormones from the adrenal cortex.

(d) The sympathetic nervous system is responsible for stimulating the release of epinephrine and norepinephrine from the adrenal medulla. The adrenal medulla is, in fact, a modified sympathetic ganglion.

Neurohormones (page 121)

1. (a) The anterior pituitary is glandular and secretes hormones in response to releasing hormones from the hypothalamus. The posterior pituitary is neural in origin and simply stores and releases neurohormones that originate in the hypothalamic neurosecretory cells.

(b) The posterior pituitary secretes neurohormones from modified secretory neurons, whereas the anterior pituitary secretes peptide hormones when influenced by other hormonal signals.

2. Neurosecretory cells in the hypothalamus produce oxytocin and ADH which are stored in, and released from, the posterior pituitary. Other neurohormones secreted by the hypothalamus control the release of hormones from the anterior pituitary.

3. The adrenal and thyroid glands rely on the influence of regulatory hormones from the anterior pituitary. Without the input of these hormones, there is no stimulation of the glands and they become underactive and atrophy.

4 The hypothalamus controls the activity of the hormonal secretion from the pituitary. Without its regulatory input, the pituitary would cease to function.

The Stress Response (page 122)

1. The body's short term response to stress is adaptive because it readies the body for the extra work it might have to do in terms of increased breathing rate, heart rate, and muscular activity. It prepares the body to most efficiently flee or defend itself.

2. (a) A prolonged period of stress triggers release of ACTH from the pituitary (mediated by the hypothalamus) and brings about the release of glucocorticoids from the adrenal cortex. These mediate suppression of the immune system and metabolism of fats and proteins, which helps the body to direct its efforts towards maintaining activity throughout the stressful period.

(b) Unrelieved stress leads to elevated levels of glucocorticoids (especially cortisol) which leads to prolonged immune suppression, lowered resistance to disease, and elevated levels of blood sugar. Eventually, the capacity of glands and the immune system is exhausted making the subject susceptible to illnesses such as ulcers, depression, diabetes, digestive trouble, and cardiovascular disease.

Hormones of the Pituitary (page 123)

1 (a) Growth hormone has generally anabolic effects. It stimulates the proliferation of chondrocytes and deposition of bone, it stimulates muscle growth through protein synthesis and proliferation of myoblasts, and it promotes the utilization of fats.

(b) Chronic or total growth hormone deficiency in infancy results in the child being small, with an immature face and chubby body build. Rate of growth of all body parts is slow so that the child's proportions remain normal.

(c) In the rare case of chronic hypersecretion of growth hormone in infancy, the child exhibits rampant growth or gigantism (a condition called acromegaly).

(d) Secretion of GH hormone is regulated through (1) negative feedback of IGF-1 to suppress secretion of GnRH from the hypothalamus and (2) high levels of IGF-1 stimulating release of hypothalamic somatostatin which also supresses GH secretion.

2. The pituitary produces GH and TSH. TSH controls the release of hormones from the thyroid which are involved in the regulation of metabolic rate. GH stimulates the liver and other tissues to secrete IGF-1, which is both an endocrine and an autocrine/paracrine hormone and mediates the metabolic effects attributable to GH (see 1a).

3. Release of TSH is controlled by a regulating factor, thyrotropin releasing factor (hormone) or TRF(TRH) from the hypothalamus. Low levels of thyroid hormones or low metabolic rate stimulate release of TRF from the hypothalamus. TRF stimulates release of TSH (and increase secretion of thyroid hormones). When normal thyroid hormone levels are restored, TRF release stops.

4. Iodine deficiency results in the thyroid swelling because TSH is stimulating the gland to make thyroxin and T_3. This condition is called goiter. **Note**: Iodine deficiency is also responsible for some cases of thyroid underactivity (hypothyroidism).

Control of Blood Glucose (page 125)

1. (a) Stimulus: Rise in the levels of glucose in the blood above a set level (about 5.5 mmol per L).

(b) Stimulus: Fall in blood glucose levels below a set level (about 3.5 mmol per L).

(c) Glucagon brings about the production (and subsequent release) of glucose from the liver by the breakdown of glycogen and synthesis of glucose from amino acids.

(d) Insulin increases glucose uptake by cells (thereby lowering blood glucose) and brings about production of glycogen and fat from glucose in the liver.

2. Fluctuations in blood glucose (BG) and blood insulin levels are closely aligned. Following a meal, BG rises sharply and there is a corresponding increase in blood insulin, which promotes cellular glucose uptake and a subsequent fall in BG. This pattern is repeated after each meal, with the evening meal followed by a gradual decline in BG and insulin over the sleep (fasting) period. Negative feedback mechanisms prevent excessive fluctuations in blood glucose (BG) throughout the 24 hour period.

3. Humoral.

Carbohydrate Metabolism in the Liver (page 126)

1. In any order:
(a) Glycogenesis: the production of glycogen from glucose in the liver, stimulated by insulin.
(b) Glycogenolysis: breakdown of glycogen to produce glucose, stimulated by adrenaline and glucagon.
(c) Gluconeogenesis: the production of glucose from non-carbohydrate sources, stimulated by epinephrine and glucocorticoid hormones.

2. (a) Process at 1: Glycogenesis (formation of glycogen from glucose).
(b) Process at 2: Glycogenolysis (glycogen breakdown).
(c) Process at 3: Gluconeogensis (formation of glucose from non-carbohydrate sources).

3. Interconversion of carbohydrates is essential to regulating blood glucose levels and maintaining a readily available supply of glucose as fuel without incurring the homeostatic problems of high circulating levels of glucose.

© 2009-2013 **BIOZONE** International
ISBN: 978-1-927173-59-6
Photocopying Prohibited

Type 1 Diabetes Mellitus (page 127)

1. The symptoms of Type 1 diabetes mellitus include high blood sugar and excretion of glucose in the urine, increased urine production, accelerated fat breakdown and ketosis, excessive thirst and hunger, and weight loss. These symptoms arise as a result of the lack of insulin, which is required in order for cells to take up glucose. The cells are deprived of glucose, hence the excessive hunger and loss of weight, but blood glucose is too high, hence excessive excretion of glucose, excessive urination, and excessive thirst.

2. Regular insulin injections, in combination with monitoring blood glucose levels, food intake, and activity level enables the diabetic to avoid large fluctuations in blood glucose. Insulin is delivered to enable uptake of glucose from the blood after meals, so that the detrimental effects of high blood glucose are avoided.

Type 2 Diabetes Mellitus (page 128)

1. Type 1 diabetes results from an absolute deficiency (non-production) of insulin and must be treated with insulin injection. Type 2 diabetes is a result of the body's cells becoming insensitive to insulin and ceasing to respond to normal insulin levels (usually arising as a complication of obesity). Consequently, type 2 diabetes is treated first with dietary management, exercise, and anti-diabetic drugs, with insulin therapy used only as a last resort.

2. Dietary advice centres around a reduction in caloric intake to reduce body weight, achieved through a reduction in high fat food (to reduce blood lipid levels) and an emphasis on increasing the proportion of slow energy-release (low GI) foods in order to stabilize blood sugar for longer periods.

3. An increase in type 2 diabetes is associated with the risk factors of obesity and an increasing tendency towards a sedentary lifestyle. Both these are features of developed (westernized) societies.

Alcohol, Nicotine, and Blood Glucose (page 129)

1. (a) Alcohol has a two fold effect. 1) Stimulates insulin production, promoting glucose uptake from the blood into the cells. 2) Inhibits glucagon production so the liver does not produce and release glucose in response to low blood glucose levels.
   (b) Alcohol is a metabolic toxin, so its detoxification is prioritized by the body.
2. (a) Nicotine stimulates the release of epinephrine which acts on the liver to produce glucose and on the pancreas in inhibit insulin production. The resulting increase in blood glucose is detected by the brain which reduces hunger signals.
   (b) Nicotine reduces hunger (see above). When a smoker stops, the inhibition of hunger by nicotine is removed and smokers find they are hungry more often, eat more, and put on weight.

Aging and the Endocrine System (page 130)

1. (a) Decrease in lean muscle mass (and consequent increase in fat mass).
   (b) Decrease in bone density (lower rate of bone deposition).

2. After menopause, the ovaries stop responding to FSH and LH, and estrogen levels decline. The pituitary responds to the low estrogen levels by secreting more FSH and LH in an attempt to stimulate estrogen levels. (In premenopausal women, estrogen, and LH and FSH secretion are regulated by negative feedback mechanims).

3. Loss of bone mass.

KEY TERMS: Mix and Match (page 131)
blood glucose (I), cell signaling (C), cyclic AMP (G), diabetes mellitus (T), endocrine gland (K), exocrine gland (R), glucagon (O), hormone (B), hypothalamus (E), insulin (A), menopause (H), negative feedback (Q), neurosecretory cell (P), pancreas (F), pituitary gland (N), positive feedback (S), second messenger (M), signal molecule (J), signal transduction pathway (D), target cell (L).

The Human Transport System (page 135)

1. (a) Head
   (b) Lungs
   (c) Liver
   (d) Gut (intestines)
   (e) Kidneys
   (f) Genitals/lower body

Arteries (page 136)

1. (a) Tunica externa
   (b) Tunica media
   (c) Endothelium
   (d) Blood (or lumen)

2. (a) Thick, elastic walls are required in order to withstand the high pressure of the blood being pumped from the heart. **Note:** The elasticity also helps to even out the surges that occur with each contraction of the heart. This keeps the blood moving forward in a continuous flow.
   (b) Blood pressure is low within the arterioles.

3. The smooth muscle around arteries helps to regulate blood flow and pressure. By contracting or relaxing it alters the diameter of the artery and adjusts the volume of blood as required.

4. (a) The diameter of the artery increases.
   (b) The blood pressure decreases.

Veins (page 137)

1. (a) Veins have less elastic and muscle tissue than arteries.
   (b) Veins have a larger lumen than arteries.

2. Most of the structural differences between arteries and veins are related to the different blood pressures inside the vessels. Blood in veins travels at low pressure and veins do not need to be as strong, hence the thinner layers of muscle and elastic tissue and the relatively larger lumen.

3. Veins are "massaged" by the skeletal muscles (e.g. leg muscles). Valves (together with these muscular movements) help to return venous blood to the heart by preventing backflow away from the heart. **Extra note**: When skeletal muscles contract and tighten around a vein the valves open and blood is driven towards the heart. When the muscles relax, the valves close, preventing backflow.

4. Venous blood oozes out in an even flow from a wound because it has lost a lot of pressure after passing through the narrow capillary vessels (with their high resistance to flow). Arterial blood spurts out rapidly because it is being pumped directly from the heart and has not yet entered the capillary networks.

Capillaries (page 138)

1. **Capillaries** are very small blood vessels forming networks that penetrate all parts of the body. The only tissue present is an endothelium of squamous epithelial cells. In contrast, **arteries** have a thin endothelium, a central layer of elastic tissue and smooth muscle and a thick outer layer of elastic and connective tissue. **Veins** have a thin endothelium, a central layer of elastic and muscle tissue and a thin outer layer of elastic connective tissue. Veins also have valves.

2. (a) Sinusoids differ from capillaries in that they are wider and follow a more convoluted path through the tissue. They are lined with phagocytic cells rather than the usual endothelial lining of capillaries.
   (b) Capillaries and sinusoids are similar in that they both transport blood from arterioles to venules.

Capillary Networks (page 139)

1. Capillaries are branching networks of fine blood vessels where exchanges between blood and tissue take place. Blood enters the network at the arteriolar end and is collected by venues at the venous end. The true capillaries

form a network outside of the vascular shunt.

2. The smooth muscle sphincters regulate the blood flow to the capillary network by contracting to restrict blood flow to the network and relaxing to allow blood to flow in. The vascular shunt connects the arteriole and venule and allows blood to bypass the capillaries when the smooth muscle sphincters are contracted.

3. (a) Situation A would occur when the body is restricting blood flow to the capillaries, for example when trying to conserve heat by diverting blood away from the extremities.
   (b) Situation B would occur when the body is trying to remove excess heat by diverting blood to the skin and extremities or when the body is trying to provide extra blood to areas of high metabolism, e.g. when exercising or digesting food.

4. A portal venous system drains blood from one capillary network into another. An example is the hepatic portal system which drains blood from the capillary network in the gut to the capillary network in the liver. Normally capillary networks drain into veins that return directly to the heart.

The Formation of Tissue Fluid (page 140)

1. The tissue fluid bathes the tissues, providing oxygen and nutrients as well as a medium for the transport (away) of metabolic wastes, e.g. CO_2.

2. Capillaries are very small blood vessels forming networks or beds that penetrate all parts of the body. Capillary walls are thin enough to allow gas exchange between the capillaries and surrounding tissue.

3. (a) Arteriolar end: Hydrostatic pressure predominates in causing fluid to move out of the capillaries.
   (b) Venous end: Increased concentration of solutes and reduction in hydrostatic pressure at the venous end of a capillary bed lowers the solute potential within the capillary and there is a tendency for water and solutes to re-enter the capillary.

4. (a) Most tissue fluid finds it way directly back into the capillaries as a result of net inward pressure at the venule end of the capillary bed.
   (b) The lymph vessels (which parallel the blood system) drain tissue fluid (as lymph) back into the heart, thereby returning it into the main circulation.

Blood (page 141)

1. *Answers given may provide more detail than required.*
   (b) Protection against disease:
   Blood component: White blood cells
   Mode of action: Engulf bacteria, mediate immune reactions, and allergic and inflammatory responses.
   (c) Communication between cells, tissues and organs:
   Blood component: Hormones
   Mode of action: Specific chemicals which are carried in the blood to target tissues, where they interact with specific receptors and bring about an appropriate response.
   (d) Oxygen transport:
   Blood component: Hemoglobin molecule of erythrocytes.
   Mode of action: Binds oxygen at the lungs and releases it at the tissues.
   (e) Carbon dioxide transport:
   Blood components: Mainly plasma (most carbon dioxide is carried as bicarbonate in the plasma, a small amount is dissolved in the plasma). Red blood cells (a small amount (10-20%) of carbon dioxide is carried bound to hemoglobin).
   Mode of action: Diffuses between tissues, plasma, and lungs according to concentration gradient.
   (f) Buffer against pH changes:
   Blood components: Hemoglobin molecule of erythrocytes. Plasma bicarbonate and proteins.
   Mode of action: Free hydrogen ions are picked up and carried by the hemoglobin molecule (removed from solution). Plasma bicarbonate can form either carbonic acid by picking up a hydrogen ion (H^+), or sodium bicarbonate by combining with sodium ions. Negatively

charged proteins also associate with H^+.
   (g) Nutrient supply:
   Blood component: Plasma
   Mode of action: Glucose is carried in the plasma and is taken up by cells (made available throughout the body to all tissues).
   (h) Tissue repair:
   Blood components: Platelets and leukocytes
   Mode of action: Platelets initiate the cascade of reactions involved in clotting and wound repair. Leukocytes (some types) engulf bacteria and foreign material, preventing or halting infection.
   (i) Hormone, lipid, and fat soluble vitamin transport:
   Blood component: α-globulins
   Mode of action: α-globulins bind these substances and carry them in the plasma. This prevents them being filtered in the kidneys and lost in the urine.

2. Any of: Presence (WBC) or absence (RBC) of **nucleus**. Color, reflecting presence (RBC) or absence (WBC) of respiratory pigment, **hemoglobin**. **Shape and size** (smaller, dish shaped RBCs vs larger, rounded WBCs. **Mitochondria** present in WBCs, absent in RBCs.

3. (a) Lack of a nucleus allows more space in the cell to carry Hb (hence greater O_2 carrying capacity).
   (b) Lack of mitochondria forces the red blood cells to metabolize anaerobically so that they do not consume the oxygen they are carrying.

4. (a) Elevated eosinophil count: Allergic response such as hay fever or asthma.
   (b) Elevated neutrophil count: Microbial infection
   (c) Elevated basophil count: Inflammatory response e.g. as a result of an allergy or a parasitic (as opposed to bacterial) infection.
   (d) Elevated lymphocyte count: Infection or response to vaccination.

Hematopoiesis (page 143)

1. (a) Fetal liver.   (b) Red bone marrow.

2. (a) Myeloid progenitor cells: megakaryocyte (and platelets), monocytes, macrophages, granulocytes, red blood cells.
   (b) Lymphoid progenitor cells: T lymphocytes, B lymphocytes, and NK lymphocytes.

3. The main purpose of ASC are to maintain and repair the tissue in which they are found. Examples are:
   – Hematopoietic stem cells give rise to all the types of blood cells, red blood cells, lymphocytes, leukocytes and platelets.
   – Bone marrow stromal cells (mesenchymal stem cells) give rise to a variety of cell types including bone cells (osteocytes), cartilage cells (chondrocytes), fat cells (adipocytes) and connective tissue cells such as tendons.
   – Neural stem cells in the brain can produce nerve cells (neurons) and the non-neuronal cells astrocytes and oligodendrocytes.
   – Epithelial stem cells that line the digestive tract give rise to absorptive cells, globet cells, Paneth cells and enteroendocrine cells.
   – Skin stem cells in the basal layer of the epidermis form keratinocytes which protect the skin. Follicular stem cells at the base of hair follicles give rise to the hair follicle and epidermal cells.
   (b) Skin, stem cells in the brain, digestive tract (as described in more detail in (a) above).
   (c) Blood cells have a short life in circulation as opposed to other cells, such as neurons, which are long-lived.

Exercise and Blood Flow (page 144)

1. Answers for missing values are listed from top to bottom under the appropriate heading:

	At rest (% of total)	Exercise (% of total)
Heart	4.0	4.2
Lung	2.0	1.1
Kidneys	22.0	3.4
Liver	27.0	3.4
Muscle	15.0	70.2

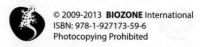

© 2009-2013 **BIOZONE** International
ISBN: 978-1-927173-59-6
Photocopying Prohibited

Bone	5.0	1.4
Skin	6.0	10.7
Thyroid	1.0	0.3
Adrenals	0.5	0.1
Other	3.5	1.0

2. The heart beats faster and harder to increase the volume of blood pumped per beat and the number of beats per minute (increased blood flow).

3. (a) Blood flow increases approximately 3.5 times.
   (b) Working tissues require more oxygen and nutrients than can be delivered by a resting rate of blood flow. Therefore the rate of blood flow (delivery to the tissues) must increase during exercise.

4. (a) Thyroid and adrenal glands, as well as the tissues other than those defined in the table, show no change in absolute rate of blood flow.
   (b) This is because they are not involved in exercise and do not require an increased blood flow. However, they need to maintain their usual blood supply and cannot tolerate an absolute decline.

5. (a) Skeletal muscles (increases 16.7X), skin (increases 6.3X), and heart (increases 3.7X)
   (b) These tissues and organs are all directly involved in the exercise process and need a greater rate of supply of oxygen and nutrients. Skeletal muscles move the body, the heart must pump a greater volume of blood at a greater rate and the skin must help cool the body to maintain core temperature.

The Human Heart (page 145)

1. (a) Pulmonary artery   (e) Aorta
   (b) Vena cava   (f) Pulmonary vein
   (c) Right atrium   (g) Left atrium
   (d) Right ventricle   (h) Left ventricle

Positions of heart valves

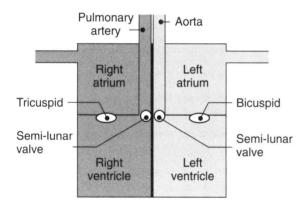

2. **Valves** prevent the blood from flowing the wrong way through the heart and help regulate filling of the chambers.

3. (a) The heart has its own coronary blood supply to meet the heart tissue's high oxygen demands.
   (b) There must be a system within the heart muscle itself to return deoxygenated blood and waste products of metabolism back to the right atrium.

4. If blood flow to a particular part of the heart is restricted or blocked (because of blocked blood vessel), the part of the heart muscle supplied by that vessel will die, leading to a heart attack or infarction.

5. A: arterioles   B: venules
   C: arterioles   D: capillaries

6. (a) The pulmonary circuit must operate at a lower pressure than the systemic circuit to prevent fluid accumulation in the lungs. The systemic circuit must also develop enough pressure to enable blood flow to increase to the muscles when required and to maintain kidney filtration rates without compromising blood supply to the brain.
   (b) The left ventricle is thicker to enable the left side of

the heart to develop higher pressure. There is no such requirement of the right side, which pumps only to through the lower pressure pulmonary circuit.

7. You are recording expansion and recoil of the artery that occurs with each contraction of the left ventricle.

The Cardiac Cycle (page 147)

1. (a) QRS complex   (b) T   (c) P

2. During the period of electrical recovery the heart muscle cannot contract. This ensures that the heart has an enforced rest and will not fatigue, nor accumulate lactic acid (as occurs in working skeletal muscle).

3. Extra text removed and letter answers have been placed for each cycle.

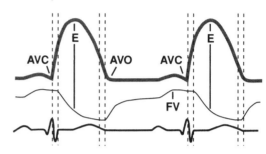

Dissecting a Mammalian Heart (page 148)

1.

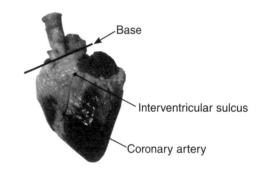

2. Vena cava.

3. Aorta.

4. Pulmonary artery.

5. Chordae tendinae (also spelt chordae tendineae) hold the valves between the atrium and ventricle closed during contraction of the ventricle.

6. The thickness of the ventricle walls (the right ventricle wall is relatively thin while the left ventricle wall is much thicker and very muscular).

The Intrinsic Regulation of Heartbeat (page 150)

1. (a) **Sinoatrial node**: Initiates cardiac cycle through the spontaneous generation of action potentials.
   (b) **Atrioventricular node**: Delays the impulse.
   (c) **Bundle of His**: Distributes action potentials over the ventricles (resulting in ventricular contraction).
   (d) **Intercalated discs**: Specialized junctions allowing electrical impulses to spread rapidly through the heart muscle (electrical coupling).

2. Delaying the impulse at the AVN allows time for atrial contraction to finish before the ventricles contract.

3. (a) Heart muscle contracts more strongly when stretched.
   (b) Response enables it to cope with an increased blood volume, i.e. increased venous return as during exercise.

© 2009-2013 **BIOZONE** International
ISBN: 978-1-927173-59-6
Photocopying Prohibited

Extrinsic Control of Heart Rate (page 151)

1. (a) **Increased venous return**: Heart rate increases.
   (b) **Release of epinephrine**: Heart rate increases.
   (c) **Increase in blood CO_2**: Heart rate increases.

2. These effects are mediated through the cardiovascular center (sympathetic output via the cardiac nerve).

3. Physical exercise increases venous return (blood returning at a faster rate to the heart).

4. (a) Cardiac nerve.
   (b) Erratum: Question should read...brings about **decreased** heart rate". Vagus nerve.

5. Increased stretch in the vena cava indicates increased venous return and cardiac output must increase to cope with the increase. Increased stretch in the aorta indicates increased cardiac output and heart rate decreases The two responses keep cardiac output regulated according to the body's requirement.

Stress and Heart Rate (page 152)

1. (a) Sympathetic nervous stimulation increases the rate and force of heart contraction.
   (b) Epinephrine and norepinephrine.

2. Elevated heart rate increases cardiac output, supplying more blood to muscles in preparation for responding to the stress (e.g. running or fighting).

3. Norepinephrine is released from the axon terminals of the sympathetic (cardiac) nerve and acts as a neurotransmitter to increase heart rate. Norepinephrine is also released from sympathetic nerves supplying the adrenal medulla, stimulating release of norepinephrine (and epinephrine) which act as hormones to increase cardiac output.

4. (a) When the stress is removed, there is reuptake of epinephrine and norepinephrine into the nerve endings. These catecholamines are also metabolized.
   (b) Unresolved stress leads to elevated levels of epinephrine and norepinephrine and results in detrimentally elevated heart rate, blood glucose, nervous tension etc. Note that epinephrine and norepinephrine (unlike most other hormones) do not down-regulate their own secretion by negative feedback.

Review of the Human Heart (page 153)

1. (A) Cardiac nerve (sympathetic nerve is acceptable).
   (B) Baroreceptors in the vena cava and right atrium.
   (C) Vagus nerve (parasympathetic nerve is acceptable).
   (D) Aortic baroreceptors.
   (1) Sinoatrial node (SAN).
   (2) Atrioventricular node (AVN).
   (3) Bundle of His (atrioventricular bundle).
   (4) Right ventricle.
   (5) Pulmonary artery.
   (6) Left atrium.
   (7) Purkyne fibers (aka Purkinje fibers).
   (8) Left ventricle.

2. A = Contraction of the atria.
   B = Contraction of the ventricles.
   C = Relaxation and recovery of ventricles.

3. (a)

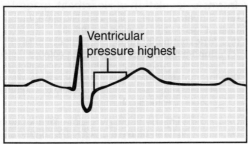

   Ventricular pressure highest

   (b) Ventricular volume is decreasing.

Investigating Cardiovascular Physiology (page 154)

The answer students will get to this activity depends on their own cardiovascular fitness.

The Effects of Aerobic Training (page 155)

1. (a) **Training**: The stress generated by repeated exercise of a certain duration and intensity.
   (b) The body adjusts to the training stress by altering its physiology in such a way that the impact of future stress is minimized.

2. (a) **Increase in stroke volume and cardiac output**: Increases the volume of blood transported to and from the working tissues.
   (b) **Increased ventilation efficiency**: Increases the rate of gas exchange (oxygen transported into and carbon dioxide transported out of the blood).
   (c) **Increased capillary density in muscle tissue**: Increased capacity for oxygen supply to working muscle (and therefore oxidative metabolism) as well as improved removal of metabolic wastes.

3. Heart size increases because (like any muscle) it gets bigger with work. The larger size also means it pumps a greater volume of blood more efficiently.

4. Endurance athletes have a smaller body weight.

5. With each stroke, the heart pumps a larger volume of blood. Less energy is expended in pumping the same volume of blood.

6. A lower resting pulse (=heart rate) means that for most of the time, the heart is not working as hard as in someone with a higher resting pulse. On average, over a long period of time, the heart works less for any given amount of effort.

Cardiovascular Disease (page 157)

1. Cardiovascular disease (CVD) refers to a class of diseases affecting the cardiovascular system (heart or blood vessels).

2. Certain behavioral or lifestyle factors are strongly correlated with the risk of developing and dying from CVD. Many people living in western countries are overweight or obese, they consume foods high in fat, salt, and sugar, and do not consume enough fruit and vegetables a day. In addition, many people are not meeting recommended activity levels. These lifestyle factors makes a person more susceptible to developing and dying from CVD. CVD is also a 'silent killer', it is possible to develop CVD without realizing it until it is too late (e.g a person has a fatal heart attack or stroke).

3. Congenital defects are defects that a person is born with. They can be inherited, the result of viral infections, or the result of genetic defects (mutations). In contrast, contracted defects arise during the course of a person's life. They are mostly caused by environment or lifestyle factors, but can sometimes be the result of genetics.

Atherosclerosis (page 158)

1. Even though a plaque is forming, blood can continue to flow relatively unhindered through blood vessels. It is only when the blood vessel is almost completely closed that symptoms arise. Fit, healthy people may not show any symptoms at all until a plaque ruptures and causes a major blood clot, which can be lethal.

2. Atherosclerosis is triggered when a vessel is damaged (e.g. by persistent hypertension). LDLs accumulate at the damaged site and macrophages follow forming foam cells. The foam cells accumulate to form an intermediate lesion called a plaque. As the atheroma develops, the smooth muscle cells of the blood vessel die, and scar tissue forms. Calcium salts accumulate forming and a complicated plaque and the arterial wall may ulcerate. The plaque may break away forming a clot, which may be fatal.

3. People with atherosclerosis are more at risk of suffering an aneurysm, stroke, or heart attack. This is because their blood vessels may become blocked from the plaque or by a blood clot resulting from an atherosclerotic plaque which has broken off as a blood clot.

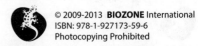

© 2009-2013 **BIOZONE** International
ISBN: 978-1-927173-59-6
Photocopying Prohibited

CVD Risk Factors (page 159)

1. (a) Controllable risk factors for CVD are those that can be altered by changing diet or other lifestyle factors, or by controlling a physiological disease state (e.g. high blood pressure, or high blood cholesterol). Uncontrollable risk factors are those over which no control is possible, e.g. genetic predisposition, sex, or age. Note that the impact of uncontrollable factors can be reduced by changing controllable factors.
    (b) Controllable risk factors often occur together because some tend to be causative for others, or at least always associated, e.g. obesity greatly increases the risk of high blood lipids and high blood pressure: all factors increase risk of CVD.
    (c) The data show that those with several risk factors have a higher chance of developing CVD. This is because the risks are cumulative and sum to produce a greater total risk. For example, judging by the rate of CHD, the risk if a person (male or female) has 6 risk factors (elevated systolic BP, elevated total cholesterol and low HD cholesterol, diabetes, smoker, and ventricular enlargement) is about 5 times that of someone with only two of those risk factors (elevated systolic BP, elevated total cholesterol).

Correcting Heart Problems (page 160)

1. (a) Tissue valves: A shorter life-span means the valves require regular replacement (every 10 years or so).
    (b) Synthetic valves: Have a tendency to produce blood clots which increase the risk of stroke. Patients have long-term drug therapy to prevent clot formation.

2. Tissue valves have fewer complications associated with their use, drugs are not required to prevent rejection, and the shorter life-span of the valve is no problem in elderly patients.

3. Heart patients need careful supervision because the factors in their lifestyle that lead to the heart disease in the first instance will still be present after surgery. It is desirable that after surgery patients adopt a healthy diet, include some everyday physical activity in their routine, and try to avoid stress as much as possible.

KEY TERMS: Mix and Match (page 161)

aorta (H), artery (pl. arteries) (Q), atrioventricular (AV) node (W), atrioventricular valves (V), atrium (pl. atria) (L), blood (AA), capillary (pl. capillaries) (D), cardiac cycle (K), cardiac output (Y), cardiovascular disease (I), cardiovascular system (R), diastole (O), erythrocytes (T), heart (A), hematopoiesis (BB), leukocytes (J), lymph (E), myogenic (S), pacemaker (P), plasma (X), pulmonary artery (N), pulmonary circulation (C), pulmonary vein (F), systemic circulation (U), systole (M), vein (Z), vena cava (G), ventricle (B).

Targets for Defense (page 163)

1. The natural population of (normally non-pathogenic) microbes can benefit the host by preventing overgrowth of pathogens (by competitive exclusion).

2. (a) The **major histocompatibility complex (MHC)** is a cluster of tightly linked genes on chromosome 6 in humans. The genes code for MHC antigens (proteins) that are attached to the surfaces of all body cells and are used by the immune system to distinguish its own tissue from that which is foreign.
    (b) This self-recognition system allows the body to immediately identify foreign tissue e.g. a pathogen, and mount an immune attack against it for the protection of the body's own tissues.

3. Self-recognition is undesirable:
    − **During pregnancy. Note:** Some features of the self-recognition system are disabled to enable growth (to full term) of what is essentially a large foreign body.
    − **During tissue and organ grafts/transplants** from another human (allografting) or a non-human animal (xenografting). **Note:** Such grafts are usually for the purpose of replacing rather than repairing tissue (e.g. grafting to replace damaged heart valves). The self-

recognition system must also be suppressed indefinitely by immunosuppressant drugs.

Autoimmune Diseases (page 164)

1. (a) **Multiple sclerosis**: An autoimmune disorder in which the T-lymphocytes and monocytes target and destroy the myelin sheath around neurons.
    (b) **Rheumatoid arthritis**: An inflammatory joint disease caused by autoimmune destruction of cartilage. Lymphocytes are activated and cytokinins are expressed in the inflamed areas.

2. **Autoimmune diseases** are difficult to treat effectively because the trigger of the disease is often unknown and each disease can affect the body in a different way. **Note:** Of the two types of autoimmune disorders, organ-specific and non-organ specific, the latter is the more difficult to treat because it is spread widely throughout the body.

3. **AIDS** sufferers develop a range of debilitating infections because their immune system is already compromised and they are unable to fight off even minor infections.

Blood Group Antigens (page 165)

1. Completed table:

Blood type	Antigen	Antibody	Can donate to:	Can receive blood from:
A	A	anti-B	A, AB	A, O
B	B	anti-A	B, AB	B, O
AB	A + B	none	AB	A, B, AB, O
O	None	anti-A + anti-B	O, AB, A, B	O

2. Blood from an incompatible donor contains RBC antigens which react with the pre-formed antibodies of the recipient. These antibodies cause the donor blood's RBCs to clump together, block capillaries and rupture.

3. **Correction: Blood type should read O⁻**
    (People with) O⁻ blood are sometimes called universal donors because they can donate blood to all other blood types (their red blood cells have no antigens including no Rh antigens).

4. (People with) AB⁺ blood are sometimes called universal recipients because they lack antibodies to either the A or B antigens, and to Rh antigens, and can therefore receive blood from all blood types (with AB preferred).

5. Discovery of the basis of the ABO system allowed the possibility of **safe** transfusions and greatly improved survival and recovery after surgery or trauma.

Blood Clotting and Defense (page 166)

1. (a) Prevents bleeding and invasion of bacteria.
    (b) Aids in the maintenance of blood volume.

2. (a) Injury exposes collagen fibers to the blood.
    (b) Chemicals make the surrounding platelets sticky.
    (c) Clumping forms an immediate plug of platelets preventing blood loss.
    (d) Fibrin clot traps red blood cells and reinforces the seal against blood loss.

3. (a) Clotting factors catalyze the conversion of prothrombin to thrombin, the active enzyme that catalyzes the production of fibrin.
    (b) If clotting factors were always present, clotting could not be contained; blood would clot when it shouldn't.

4. (a) and (b) provided below. The first is the obvious answer, but there are disorders associated with the absence of each of the twelve clotting factors:
    (a) Classic hemophilia

© 2009-2013 **BIOZONE** International
ISBN: 978-1-927173-59-6
Photocopying Prohibited

(b) Clotting factor VIII (anti-hemophilic factor)
(a) Hemophilia B (Christmas disease)
(b) Clotting factor IX (Christmas factor).

The Body's Defenses (page 167)

1. **Specific** resistance refers to defense against particular (identified) pathogens. It involves a range of specific responses to the pathogen concerned (antibody production and cell-mediated immunity). In contrast, **non-specific** resistance refers to defense against any type of pathogen.

2. The skin provides a physical barrier to prevent pathogens entering the body. Skin secretions (serum and sweat) contain antimicrobial chemicals which inhibit microbial growth.

3. (a) Phospholipases kill bacteria by hydrolysing the phospholipids in cell walls and membranes.
   (b) Cilia moves the microbes, which are trapped in mucus towards the mouth and nostrils., where they can be expelled.
   (c) Sebum has antimicrobial activity and (with sweat) a pH that is unfavorable for microbial growth.

4. (a) Phagocytosis destroys pathogens directly by engulfing them.
   (b) Antimicrobial substances (e.g. interferon) prevent multiplication of microbes (especially viruses).
   (c) Antibodies are produced against specific pathogens, and bind and destroy pathogens or their toxins.

5. A hierarchical system of defense provides a series of back-ups in case a pathogen breaches earlier barriers. Most microbes are excluded by the first line of defense, but those that penetrate the skin will usually be destroyed by white blood cells and the chemicals associated with inflammation. Failing this, the body will mount a targeted specific defense against the identified pathogen still remaining.

The Action of Phagocytes (page 169)

1. Neutrophils, eosinophils, macrophages.

2. By looking at the ratio of white blood cells to red blood cells (not involved in the immune response). An elevated white blood cell count (specifically a high neutrophil count) indicates microbial infection.

3. Microbes may be able to produce toxins that kill phagocytes directly. Others can enter the phagocytes, completely filling them and preventing them functioning or remaining dormant and resuming activity later.

Inflammation (page 170)

1. (a) Increased diameter and permeability of blood vessels. **Role**: Increases blood flow and delivery of leukocytes to the area. Aids removal of destroyed microbes or their toxins. Allows defensive substances to leak into the tissue spaces.
   (b) Phagocyte migration and phagocytosis. **Role**: To directly attack and destroy invading microbes and foreign substances.
   (c) Tissue repair. **Role**: Replaces damaged cells and tissues, restoring the integrity of the area.

2. Ability to squeeze through capillary walls (amoeboid movement). Ability to engulf material by phagocytosis.

3. Histamines and prostaglandins attract phagocytes to the site of infection.

4. Pus is the accumulated debris of infection (dead phagocytes, damaged tissue, and fluid). It accumulates at the site of infection where the defense process is most active.

Fever (page 171)

1. The high body temperature associated with fever intensifies the action of interferon (a potent antiviral substance). Fever also increases metabolism, which is associated with increased blood flow. These changes increase the rate at which white blood cells are delivered to the site of infection

and help to speed up the repair of tissues. The release of interleukin-1 during fever helps to increase the production of T cell lymphocytes and speeds up the immune response.

2. **1**: Macrophage ingests a microbe and destroys it.
   2: The release of endotoxins from the microbe induces the macrophage to produce interleukin-1 which is released into the blood.
   3: Interleukin-1 travels in the blood to the hypothalamus of the brain where it stimulates the production of large amounts of prostaglandins.
   4: Prostaglandins cause resetting of the thermostat to a higher temperature, causing fever.

The Lymphatic System (page 172)

1. **Lymph** has a similar composition to tissue fluid but has more leukocytes (derived from lymphoid tissues). **Note**: Tissue fluid is similar in composition to plasma (i.e. containing water, ions, urea, proteins, glucose etc.) but lacks the large proteins found in plasma.

2. Lymph returns tissue fluid to general circulation and (with the blood) circulates lymphocytes around the body.

3. (a) **Lymph nodes**: Filter foreign material from the lymph by trapping it in fibers. They also produce lymphocytes.
   (b) **Bone marrow**: Produce many kinds of white blood cells: monocytes, macrophages, neutrophils, eosinophils, basophils, T and B lymphocytes.

The Immune System (page 173)

1. (a) **Humoral immune system**: Production of antibodies against specific antigens. The antibodies disable circulating antigens.
   (b) **Cell-mediated immune system**: Involves the production of T cells, which destroy pathogens or their toxins by direct contact or by producing substances that regulate the activity of other cells in the immune system.

2. The presence of an antigen results in the proliferation of specific types of B- and T-cell to target that antigen. Cytokines are also released by macrophages which enhance T-cell activation. More cytokines are released by activated T-cells, and this causes proliferation of other helper T-cells and B-cells.

Clonal Selection (page 174)

1. Millions of B-cells form during development. Each B-cell recognises one antigen only, and produces antibodies against it. A pathogen will trigger a response in the B-cell specific that is for it, resulting in proliferation of that B-cell. This is called clonal selection (the antigen selects the B-cell clone that will proliferate).

2. (a) Memory cells retain an antigen memory. They rapidly differentiate into antibody-producing plasma cells if they come across the same antigen again.
   (b) Plasma cells secrete antibodies against antigens (very rapid rate of antibody production).

3. (a) Immunological memory is the result of the differentiation of B cells after the first exposure to an antigen. Those B cells that differentiate into long-lived memory cells are present to react quickly in the event of a second infection..
   (b) During development, any B cells that react to the body's own antigens are selectively destroyed. This process leads to self tolerance. It is important that the immune system can distinguish self from non-self so it does not destroy its own tissue.

Antibodies (page 175)

1. **Antibodies** are proteins produced in response to antigens; they recognize and bind antigens. **Antigens** are foreign substances (often proteins) that promote the formation of antibodies (invoke an immune response).

© 2009-2013 **BIOZONE** International
ISBN: 978-1-927173-59-6
Photocopying Prohibited

2. (a) The immune system must distinguish self from non-self in order to recognize foreign material (and destroy it) and its own tissue (and not destroy it).
   (b) During development, any B cells that react to the body's own antigens are selectively destroyed. This process leads to **self tolerance**.
   (c) Autoimmune disease (disorder).
   (d) Any two of: Grave's disease (thyroid enlargement), rheumatoid arthritis (primarily joint inflammation), insulin-dependent diabetes mellitus (caused by immune destruction of the insulin-secreting cells in the pancreas), hemolytic anemia (premature destruction of red blood cells), and probably multiple sclerosis (destruction of myelin around nerves).

3. Antibodies inactivate pathogens in four main ways: **Neutralization** describes the way in which antibodies bind to viral binding sites and bacterial toxins and stop their activity. Antibodies may also **inactivate particulate antigens**, such as bacteria, by sticking them together in clumps. Soluble antigens may be bound by antibodies and fall out of solution (**precipitation**) so that they lose activity. Antibodies also activate **complement** (a defense system involving serum proteins), tagging foreign cells so that they can be recognized and destroyed.

4. (a) **Phagocytosis**: Antibodies promote the formation of inactive clumps of foreign material that can easily be engulfed and destroyed by a phagocytic cell.
   (b) **Inflammation**: Antibodies are involved in activation of complement (the defense system involving serum proteins which participate in the inflammatory response and other immune system activities).
   (c) **Bacterial cell lysis**: Antibodies are involved in tagging foreign cells for destruction and in the activation of complement (the defense system involving serum proteins which participate in the lysis of foreign cells).

Acquired Immunity (page 177)

1. (a) Passive immunity describes the immunity that develops after antibodies are transferred from one person to another. The recipient does not make the antibodies themselves.
   (b) Naturally acquired passive immunity arises as a result of antibodies passing from the mother to the fetus/infant via the placenta/breast milk. Artificially acquired passive immunity arises as a result of injection with immune serums e.g. in antivenoms.

2. (a) Newborns need to be supplied with maternal antibodies because they have not yet had exposure to the common microbes in their environment and must be born with operational defense mechanisms.
   (b) Breast milk provides a continued antibody supply that is updated according to the local environment. **Extra explanation**: It takes time for the infant's immune system to become fully functional. After birth, the supply of antibodies received during pregnancy declines. Breast milk boosts antibody levels while the infant's immune system matures.
   (c) Yes. Breast feeding will provide the infant with a naturally acquired passive immunity to help protect it against infections while its immune system develops. Without this acquisition, the infant is more vulnerable to everyday infections against which you already have immunity but he/she does not.

3. (a) Active immunity is immunity that develops after the body has been exposed to a microbe or its toxins and an immune response has been invoked.
   (b) Naturally acquired active immunity arises as a result of exposure to an antigen such as a pathogen, e.g. natural immunity to chickenpox. Artificially acquired active immunity arises as a result of vaccination, e.g. any childhood disease for which vaccinations are given: diphtheria, measles, mumps, polio etc.

4. (a) The primary response is less pronounced (smaller magnitude) than the secondary response, takes longer to develop, and is over more quickly than the secondary response. The secondary response involves a much more rapid response in antibody production, and to a

much higher level. The secondary response is much stronger and also much longer lasting.
   (b) The immune system has been prepared to respond to the antigen by the first exposure to it. When the cells of the immune system receive a second exposure to the same antigen they are able to quickly respond with the rapid production of antibodies.

5. (a) Herd immunity refers to the protection that unimmunized people have against a circulating disease by virtue of the fact that most of the population are immunized.
   (b) A fall in vaccination rates is a concern because, once the population contains a high proportion of non-vaccinated people, herd immunity is lost and a circulating disease can spread very rapidly through the community, raising public health costs and contributing to lost productivity.

Vaccines and Vaccination (page 179)

1. Attenuated viruses are more effective in the long term because they tend to replicate in the body, and the original dose therefore increases over time. Such vaccines are derived from mutations accumulated over time in a laboratory culture, so there is always a risk that they will back-mutate to a virulent form.

2. High vaccination rates increase the rates of immunity within a population, so fewer people will contract the disease with each outbreak. Transmission of the disease is limited because there are fewer susceptible hosts for the disease to exploit, until eventually the disease no longer occurs in the population.

3. (a) Introducing the whooping cough vaccine in the 1940s greatly reduced the number of cases of whooping cough contracted each year in the US.
   (b) Whooping cough immunization rates may have dropped to public perception that the vaccine was unsafe and could cause side effects such as autism.
   (c) Initially, the lower vaccination rate resulted in more cases of whooping cough. The number of whooping cough cases dropped steadily between 2005-2007, before beginning to increase again in 2008.
   (d) Herd immunity will initially provide some protection, but as overall herd immunity drops (due to decreased vaccination rates) the cases of whooping cough will begin to increase.

3. Acellular vaccines contain only fragments of the pathogen, so they are less likely to be reactive and will cause fewer side effects than whole agent vaccines. Acellular vaccines are still highly effective.

HIV and the Immune System (page 181)

1. HIV attacks the system that normally defends the body from infection. By knocking out the immune system, it leaves the body vulnerable to invasion by microbes that would not normally infect a healthy person.

2. (a) The virus rapidly increases in numbers within the first year of infection, followed by a large drop off in numbers in the second year. Over the next 3-10 years, the HIV population gradually increases again.
   (b) The helper T cell numbers respond to the initial infection by increasing in numbers. After about a year, their numbers steadily decrease as they are attacked and destroyed by the HIV.

3. **Transmission of HIV**, (a)-(c), any three of: Blood or blood products, vaginal secretions, breast milk, across the placenta, shared needles among intravenous drug users (contaminated with blood from other drug users), sexual intercourse: both homosexual (especially between males) and heterosexual (between men and women).

4. **HIV positive**: Blood tests have detected the presence of HIV in blood samples from a person (even though they may not have exhibited any symptoms).

5. Blood donated by the public and used to obtain a blood clotting factor (Factor VIII) for hemophiliacs was contaminated with HIV from donors already infected with the virus. This is particularly the case in countries where people

are paid to donate blood.

6. As a provirus, the viral DNA may remain latent (unexpressed) and replicate along with the host's DNA for some time before becoming active and transcribing its genes. This has implications for the host too, who may be unaware of infection and remain symptomless (the HIV provirus may lie dormant within a cell for varying periods of time). In addition, the virus cannot be targeted in this state without also killing the host cells. **Extra note**: There is now an HIV proviral test, which circumvents some of these issues.

Monoclonal Antibodies (page 183)

1. (a) B-lymphocyte cells.
   (b) The immune system of some people reacts against the foreign (mouse) proteins (antibodies).

2. Tumor cells are immortal and can be cultured indefinitely.

3. (a)-(d) in any order:
   (a) Diagnostic tool for detecting pathogens.
   (b) Diagnostic tool for detecting pregnancy hormones.
   (c) Neutralizing endotoxins in blood infections.
   (d) Interfering with T cell activity responsible for transplant rejection.

4. (a) Detection of bacteria or toxins in perishable food would allow the food to be disposed of rather than consumed and hence the possibility of food poisoning avoided.
   (b) Detection of pregnancy at home would give an instant result, and may circumvent a costly visit to a doctor until a pregnancy was confirmed. For some people, pregnancy detection in the privacy of their home is an attractive option.
   (c) Targeted treatment of cancerous tumors could avoid the need for more invasive or aggressive conventional cancer therapies (which have numerous, often distressing side effects).

Herceptin: A Modern Monoclonal (page 185)

1. (a) Overexpression of HER2 causes large amounts of HER2 protein, which causes the cell to divide more often than normal, producing a tumor.
   (b) HER2 protein is a normal component on the surfaces of some cells and is not recognised by the immune system as being of concern. The attachment of a foreign antibody (Herceptin) to HER2 surface proteins alerts the immune system, which then targets the Herceptin (and the HER2protein to which it is attached).

2. (a) Herceptin enables T cells to recognize cells with Her2-Herceptin complexes (i.e cancer-forming cells) and destroy them.
   (b) Herceptin blocks the cell's signa lling pathway and prevents the cell from dividing.

2. Monoclonal antibody therapies are called targeted therapies because they target only the cells with the specific antigens for the antibody involved - no others.

Allergies and Hypersensitivity (page 187)

1. Histamine mediates the symptoms of hypersensitivity reactions such as inflammation, airway constriction, and itching and watering of the eyes and nose.

2. **Sensitized**: The formation of antibodies (to an antigen) after exposure to that antigen. Once sensitized, another exposure to the antigen results in an antibody-antigen reaction (and the symptoms of an allergic response).

3. Bronchodilators dilate the bronchioles, alleviating airway constriction and allowing easier breathing.

Organ and Tissue Transplants (page 187)

1. Higher success rate of organ transplants due to:
   (a) More effective and safer drugs to suppress immune rejection of the foreign organ.
   (b) Improved techniques to match tissue type between donor and recipient.
   (c) Better techniques for organ preservation and storage (during transfer from donor).

2. (a) Organ and tissue rejection occurs because the immune system recognizes the transplanted material as foreign and sets out to destroy it.
   (b) **Immunosuppressant drugs** suppress the immune system response to foreign tissue. **Tissue typing** is important because the better the match of the histocompatibility antigens between the donor and recipient the less chance there is of immediate rejection of the transplanted material.
   (c) Drugs that suppress the immune system response can make the patient vulnerable to everyday infections. Sometimes, these may prove fatal.

3. Some points of discussion below. This answer may also take the form of a debate or a separate report. Students are unlikely to cover all issues:
   Human to human organ and tissue transplants:
   FOR:
   - Organ donation is a unique opportunity to save lives, so there is an altruistic component to donation.
   - Advances in medical technology have improved preservation techniques so that the longevity of vital organs has been improved during recovery, transport, and transplant.
   - Improvements in stem cell technology in the future will reduce the risk of rejection.
   - National and international computerized networks matching donors and recipients reduce the time it takes to locate a suitable donor.
   - Improvements in transplant technique and immunosuppressant drugs have (in some cases) more than doubled the success rate of transplants in recent years.
   - Donating tissues or organs of family members has been shown to help a bereaved family to recover from loss.
   - All major religions approve of tissue and organ transplantation.
   - In most countries, it is still a crime to gain financially from organ donation.
   - Organ transplants are now standard medical procedure; one year survival rates are good (96% (kidney), >86% (heart), 88% (liver)).
   - People of all ages can donate organs.

   AGAINST
   - Organ donation can only take place under certain circumstances (e.g. accident and brain death, or death while in intensive care). Donor must be medically and legally dead.
   - Despite advances, transplant recipients face several (avoidable) risks, including inappropriate selection and testing of donors and inadequate sterilization of some tissues. These increase the risk of infection, e.g. from prions, malignancies, and viruses such as West Nile. There is also the risk that the material for transplantation may be of poor quality (e.g. contaminated during storage or transport) and the chance of rejection therefore higher.
   - Removal of a fraction of a kidney or liver from a living donor is not risk free for the donor, especially in countries with inadequate health care facilities. There is evidence that donors themselves end up on transplant waiting lists.
   - Even well matched human transplants often fail.
   - The growing reliance on living donors creates challenges for the guiding principles of the donor programmes. Living donors must act voluntarily and without financial incentive (some policy makers want to allow payment for donation). Payment for organs increases the risk that donors will be medically unsuitable or put themselves at high risk.
   - Global safety standards are not yet in place, despite regional guidelines. Issues of donor and recipient confidentiality are still to be fully addressed.
   - Recipients need to continue with immuno-suppressant drugs to prevent transplant rejection; these have their own side effects and complications.
   - There is an widening gap between the need for organs and the number available.

© 2009-2013 **BIOZONE** International
ISBN: 978-1-927173-59-6
Photocopying Prohibited

Stem Cell Technology (page 189)

1. (a) **Self-renewal** (divide many times and stay undifferentiated) and **potency** (ability to differentiate into different cell types).

    (b) These properties mean that cell lines can be cultured indefinitely and induced to develop into particular cell types as required.

2. ESCs are pluripotent, with the correct stimulus they can differentiate into every type of cell (apart from placental tissue). As their name suggests, their only source is from embryos. ASC are multipotent, they can differentiate into a limited range of tissues, usually related to their tissue of origin. The name ASC is misleading as they are found in umbilical cord blood, children and adults. ASC are found in a limited range of tissue types (e.g. blood, skin, bone marrow).

3. ESC therapies are only undertaken in a limited research capacity. This is because the stem cells are taken from very young embryos (about five days old), which results in the destruction of an embryo. Another argument against ESC research is that it is the beginning of reproductive cloning, which many groups feel very strongly opposed to. ASC therapies are less controversial because the cells are harvested from living donors, and their removal does not cause damage or death to the donor. For this reason ASC therapies are already in use (e.g. bone marrow transplants). Note: Currently the source of embryos used in ESC research come from excess embryos created for *in vitro* fertilization. They are donated with consent to be used for the research.

4. Student's own account. **Note**: Some points of discussion are outlined below:

    Ethical issues to be considered include:
    *   The moral implications of using human embryos in an exploitative way, i.e. the embryo from which the stem cell line is derived must have been created for reproductive purposes but is subsequently discarded and must not have had the possibility of developing further as a human being.
    *   Informed consent allowing the donation of the embryo and subsequent ownership of it.
    *   Policies governing the use of the stem cell lines.

    Technically: Human embryonic stem cell (hESC) research has the potential to allow better understanding of normal cell development and subsequently the possible correction of serious medical conditions such as cancer and birth defects. Another potential application of stem cells is in making replacement cells and tissues for therapeutic purposes e.g. in treating Parkinson's and Alzheimer's diseases, spinal cord injury, stroke, burns, heart disease, diabetes, osteoarthritis and rheumatoid arthritis. Using hESCs poses formidable technical challenges as scientists must learn to control the development of pluripotent stem cells into all the different types of body cells and overcome the threat of rejection by the patient's immune system. Adult stem cell research is not new whereas hESC research is still in its infancy, lacking funding and support, and there may even be laws banning it in some countries.

Gene Therapy for Immune Dysfunction (page 191)

1. (a) The principle of gene therapy is to correct a genetic disorder of metabolism by correction, replacement, or supplementation of a faulty gene with a corrected version. **Note**: Some techniques involve culturing corrected cells *ex vivo*. Injection of corrected cells into the patient relieves the symptoms of the disorder but does cure it.

    (b) Medical areas where gene therapy might be used: Inherited genetic disorders of metabolism, cancers and other non-infectious acquired diseases, and infectious diseases (e.g. viral infections).

2. Transfection of (and correction of the genes in) **germline cells** allows the genetic changes to be inherited. **Note**: In this way, a heritable disorder can be corrected so that future generations will not carry the faulty gene(s). Transfection of **somatic cells** only corrects those cells for their lifetime.

3. **Gene amplification** is used to make multiple copies of the normal (corrective) allele.

4. SCID refers to a group of related immune system disorders affecting the production of the B and T cells responsible for the body's resistance to infection.

5. (a) Bone marrow is withdrawn from the patient and replaced with bone marrow from a compatible donor. The transplanted bone marrow stem cells produce new functional white blood cells.

    (b) The treatment is not effective for all types of SCID and there may be problems with compatibility and rejection of the marrow transplant.

    (c) Gene therapy corrects the patient's own cells so the white blood cells that develop will be their own and there will be no incompatibility issues.

5. Potential risks include:
    *   The genes may integrate randomly into chromosomes and disrupt the functioning of normal genes (this occurred recently in retroviral vectors used in SCID gene therapy).
    *   In the case of viral vectors, the host can develop a strong immune response to the viral infection. In patients disadvantaged (immune suppressed) by their disorder, this could severely undermine their health.
    *   Retroviruses infect only dividing cells, so uptake can be poor.
    *   Viruses may not survive if attacked by the host's immune system.
    *   If they do not integrate into the chromosome, the inserted genes may only function sporadically.

KEY TERMS: Mix and Match (page 193)

active immunity (N), allergies (J), antibody (I), antigen (W), artificially acquired immunity (M), B-cells (B lymphocytes) (Q), cell-mediated immunity (A), clonal selection (S), fever (Z), HIV (H), humoral immunity (F), hypersensitivity (E), immune system (T), inflammatory response (G), lymphatic system (R), major histocompatibility complex (MHC) (U), monoclonal antibodies (L), naturally acquired immunity (B), non-specific resistance (P), passive immunity (O), phagocytes (V), primary response (Y), secondary response (C), specific resistance (X), T-cells (T lymphocytes) (D), vaccination (K).

Living with Chronic Lung Disease (page 197)

1. The economic impact of tobacco smoking-related diseases is two fold. Directly there are the considerable health costs associated with treating the consequences of diseases such as chronic bronchitis and emphysema, which often require repeated and prolonged hospital visits. Secondly, there is the economic cost of lost work days (estimated 24 million lost work days per annum.

2. This response is largely a student's own and there is no 'right' answer. Tobacco-related diseases generally have a detrimental effect on a person's quality of life and on the quality of life for those who end up as carers for debilitated relatives. There are additional associated health costs with hospital and doctor's visits and treatments, and the stress of living with a chronic condition which leaves the sufferer vulnerable to more serious lung infections. Personal testimonials, such as that from Jenny's daughter, provide a first hand account of what the personal costs can be and may give some people enough reason to reconsider their smoking habit or to stop them ever taking it up.

Breathing (page 198)

1. **Breathing** ventilates the lungs, renewing the supply of fresh (high oxygen) air while expelling high carbo dioxide air (CO_2 gained as a result of gas exchanges in the tissues).

2. (a) **Quiet breathing**: External intercostal muscles and diaphragm contract. Lung space increases and air flows into the lungs (inspiration). Inflation is detected and breath in ends. Expiration occurs through elastic recoil of the ribcage and lung tissue (air flows passively out to equalize with outside air pressure).

    (b) During forced or **active breathing**, muscular contraction is involved in both the inspiration and the expiration (expiration is not passive).

3. Water vapor

© 2009-2013 **BIOZONE** International
ISBN: 978-1-927173-59-6
Photocopying Prohibited

4. The elasticity of the lung tissue enables natural recoil of the lungs during quiet breathing so that expiration is a passive process not requiring energy.

5. (a) Intrapleural pressure would increase and become the same as the intrapulmonary pressure.
   (b) The lung would collapse.

The Respiratory System (page 199)

1. (a) The structural arrangement (lobes, each with its own bronchus and dividing many times before terminating in numerous alveoli) provides an immense surface area for gas exchange.
   (b) Gas exchange takes place in the alveoli.

2. **Clarification**: Diagram should make clear that the respiratory membrane is also known as the alveolar-capillary membrane.
   The respiratory (alveolar-capillary) membrane is the layered junction between the alveolar cells, the endothelial cells of the capillaries, and their associated basement membranes. It provides a surface across which gases can freely move.

3. Surfactant reduces the surface tension of the lung tissue and counteracts the tendency of the alveoli to recoil inward and stick together after each expiration.

4. Completed table:

	Region	Cartilage	Ciliated epithelium	Goblet cells (mucus)	Smooth muscle	Connective tissue
❶	Trachea	✓	✓	✓	✓	✓
❷	Bronchus	✓	✓	✓	✓	✓
❸	Bronchioles	gradually lost	✓	✓	✓	✓
❹	Alveolar duct	✗	✗	✗	✓	✓
❺	Alveoli	✗	✗	✗	very little	✓

5. The lack of surfactant and high surface tension in the alveoli result in the collapse of the lungs to an uninflated state after each breath. **Breathing is difficult and labored**, oxygen delivery is inadequate and, **if untreated, death** usually follows in a few hours.

Measuring Lung Function (page 201)

1. (a) Taller people have larger lung volumes and capacities.
   (b) Males have larger lung volumes and capacities than females.
   (c) After adulthood, lung volume and capacity declines with age. Children have smaller lung volumes and lung capacities than adults.

2. (a) Forced volume is a more useful indicator of impairment of lung function than a tidal volume because people use only a small proportion of their lung volume in normal breathing.
   (b) Spirometry can be used to measure the extent of recovery of lung function after treatment.

3. (a) Tidal volume — vol: 0.5 L
   (b) Expiratory reserve volume — vol: 1.0 L
   (c) Residual volume — vol: 1.2 L
   (d) Inspiratory capacity — vol: 3.8 L
   (e) Vital capacity — vol: 4.8 L
   (f) Total lung capacity — vol: 6.0 L
4. **G**: Tidal volume is increasing as a result of exercise.

5. PV: 15 x 0.4 = 6 L

6. (a) During strenuous exercise, PV increases markedly.
   (b) Increased PV is achieved as a result of an increase in both breathing rate and tidal volume.

7. (a) There is 90X more CO_2 in exhaled air than in inhaled air (3.6 ÷ 0.04).
   (b) The CO_2 is the product of cellular respiration in the tissues. **Note**: Some texts give a value of 4.0% for

exhaled air (100X the CO_2 content of inhaled air).
   (c) The dead space air is not involved in gas exchange therefore retains a higher oxygen content than the air that leaves the alveoli air. This raises the oxygen content of the expired air.

Gas Transport (page 203)

1. (a) Oxygen is high in the lung alveoli and in the capillaries leaving the lung.
   (b) Carbon dioxide is high in the capillaries leaving the tissues and in the cells of the body tissues.

2. Hemoglobin binds oxygen reversibly, taking up oxygen when oxygen tensions are high (lungs), carry oxygen to where it is required (the tissues) and release it.

3. (a) As oxygen level in the blood increases, more oxygen combines with hemoglobin. However, the relationship is not linear: Hb saturation remains high even when blood oxygen levels fall very low.
   (b) When oxygen level (partial pressure) in the blood or tissues is low, hemoglobin saturation declines markedly and oxygen is released (to the tissues).

4. (a) Fetal Hb has a higher affinity for oxygen than adult Hb (it can carry 20-30% more oxygen).
   (b) This higher affinity is necessary because it enables oxygen to pass from the maternal Hb to the fetal Hb across the placenta.

5. (a) The Bohr effect.
   (b) Actively respiring tissue consumes a lot of oxygen and generates a lot of carbon dioxide. This lowers tissue pH causing more oxygen to be released from the hemoglobin to where it is required.

6. Myoglobin preferentially picks up oxygen from Hb and is able to act as an oxygen store in the muscle.

7. Any two of: **Hemoglobin**, which picks up H^+ generated by the dissociation of carbonic acid. **Bicarbonate** alone (from this dissociation), and combined with Na^+ (from the dissociation of NaCl). **Blood proteins**.

Control of Breathing (page 205)

1. The basic rhythm of breathing is controlled by the respiratory center in the medulla which sends rhythmic impulses to the intercostal muscles and diaphragm to bring about normal breathing.

2. (a) **Phrenic nerve**: Innervates the diaphragm (which contracts and moves down in inspiration).
   (b) **Intercostal nerves**: Innervate the intercostal muscles (internal and external intercostal nerves and muscles) to bring about ribcage movements.
   (c) **Vagus nerve**: Sensory portion carries impulses from stretch receptors in the bronchioles to the respiratory center to inhibit inspiration.
   (d) **Inflation reflex** (also known as the **Hering-Breuer reflex**): The inhibition of the inspiratory center to end the breath in. **Extra note**: Sensory impulses from the stretch receptors in the bronchioles travel (via the vagus) to inhibit the inspiratory center and expiration follows. When the lungs deflate, the stretch receptors are not stimulated and the inhibition of the inspiratory center stops.

3. (a) Low blood pH increases rate and depth of breathing.
   (b) Sensory information from aortic and carotid chemoreceptors is sent to the respiratory center, which mediates the increase in breathing rate. **Extra note**: Sensory impulses are sent from the carotid bodies (chemoreceptors) via the carotid sinus nerve and then the glossopharyngeal nerve. Sensory impulses from the aortic bodies (chemoreceptors) travel in the vagus nerve. Low blood pH also stimulates the chemosensitive area in the medulla directly.
   (c) Blood pH is a good indicator of high carbon dioxide levels (and therefore a need to increase respiratory rate to remove the CO_2 and obtain more oxygen).

© 2009-2013 **BIOZONE** International
ISBN: 978-1-927173-59-6
Photocopying Prohibited

Review of Lung Function (page 206)

1. (a) Nasal cavity   (i) Medullary
   (b) Oral cavity   respiratory center
   (c) Trachea   (ii) Vagus nerve
   (d) Lung   (iii) Intercostal nerve
   (e) Terminal bronchiole   (iv) Chemoreceptors
   (f) Alveoli   (v) Stretch receptors
   (g) Diaphragm   (vi) Phrenic nerve

2. A = Inspiratory reserve volume   vol: 3.3 L
   B = Inspiratory capacity   vol: 3.8 L
   C = Tidal volume   vol: 0.5 L
   D = Expiratory reserve volume   vol: 1.0 L
   Erratum: last point should be E not F
   E = Residual volume   vol: 1.2 L

Respiratory Diseases (page 207)

1. Obstructive lung diseases are those in which the air cannot reach the gas exchange region of the lung, as occurs as a result of airway constriction (asthma), excess mucus (bronchitis), or reduced lung elasticity (emphysema). Restrictive lung diseases result from scarring of the gas exchange surface (fibrosis) which results in stiffening and lack of lung expansion. Such diseases result from inhalation of dusts (e.g. coal dust).

2. (a) In a chronic obstructive pulmonary disease, the FEV_1 is reduced disproportionately more than the FVC resulting in an FEV_1/FVC ratio less than 70%.
   (b) Although the FEV_1/FVC ratio is reduced in asthmatics, there will be an improvement in the ratio towards the normal range (80%+) after treatment.
   (c) In a restrictive lung disease, both FEV1 and the FVC are compromised equally, so even though measures of lung function indicate impairment, the FEV1/FVC ratio remains high.

3. Restrictive lung diseases, such as **fibrosis**, impair lung function because the gas exchange surface becomes scarred, less flexible, and thicker. This reduces the amount of alveolar expansion possible and reduces the diffusion efficiency across the gas exchange surface.

4. Many restrictive diseases are caused by inhalation of dusts and pollutants associated with particular occupations, e.g. asbestos workers, coal miners, beryllium miners, cement workers etc.

5. In an asthma attack, histamine is released from sensitized mast cells. The histamine causes airway constriction, accumulation of fluid and mucus, and inability to breathe.

Smoking and the Lungs (page 209)

1. Long-term smoking results in increased production of mucus (in an attempt to trap and rid the lungs of smoke particles). This lung tissue is irritated and a cough develops associated with removing the excess mucus. The smoke particles indirectly destroy the alveolar walls, leading to coalescing of the alveoli and a substantial loss of lung surface area. The toxins in the smoke and tar damage the DNA of cells and lead to cancerous cells and tumors.

2. (a) **Tar**: Causes chronic irritation of the respiratory system and is also carcinogenic
   (b) **Nicotine**: Addictive component of tobacco smoke.
   (c) **Carbon monoxide**: Markedly reduces the oxygen carrying capacity of the blood by binding to haemoglobin and forming a stable carboxy-haemoglobin compound. CO has a very high affinity for Hb (higher than that of oxygen) and will preferentially occupy oxygen binding sites. It is released only slowly for the body.

3. (a) **Emphysema**: Increasing shortness of breath (which becomes increasingly more severe until it is present even at rest). Chest becomes barrel shaped (associated with air being trapped in the outer part of the lungs). Often accompanied by a chronic cough and wheeze (caused by the distension (damage and coalescing) of the alveoli). **Note**: Chronic bronchitis and emphysema are often together called chronic obstructive lung disease.
   (b) **Chronic bronchitis**: A condition in which sputum

(phlegm) is coughed up on most days during at least three consecutive months in at least two consecutive years. The disease results in widespread narrowing and obstruction of the airways in the lungs and often occurs with or contributes to emphysema.
   (c) **Lung cancer**: Impaired lung function; coughing up blood, chest pain, breathlessness, and death.

4. (a) A long term study is important with a chronic disease that develops slowly because it may take many years for convincing relationships to become evident in the data.
   (b) The study also showed that there was a convincing 20 year lag in the development of lung cancer in smokers.

Responding to Exercise (page 211)

1. (a) The output of the heart increases more than five times.
   (b) This increase is necessary because the heart must pump more blood in order to supply more oxygen to working muscles. In addition, an increased rate of blood flow ensures that metabolic waste products, which are produced at a higher rate during exercise, are removed as quickly as they are produced.
   (c) Heart and blood vessels (circulatory system).

2. (a) Oxygen consumption increases twenty times or more. Most of this increase occurs in the muscle.
   (b) An increase in metabolic activity associated with muscles working harder increases the requirements for oxygen (to supply the aerobic respiration of the muscle cells).
   (c) Resting muscles use about the same amount of oxygen as other tissues. During exercise, the muscles account for most of the total increase in oxygen consumption, i.e. the metabolic activity of the muscles increases greatly when they are working (contracting).

3. A trained athlete has a greater cardiac output (total blood flow) and a greater total oxygen consumption during exercise than an average man. The athlete's muscles adjust during training to working at a higher rate and during heavy exercise they demand more oxygen (and a higher blood flow) than the muscles of the average man. Note also that a trained athlete diverts slightly more blood (and oxygen) to the muscles at the expense of other tissues during exercise. This is a physiological adjustment made as a result of training to increase the working capacity of the muscles.

The Effects of High Altitude (page 212)

1. (a) Less oxygen is available for metabolic activity so people become breathless and often dizzy. Associated effects are headache, nausea, tiredness and coughing.
   (b) Altitude sickness or mountain sickness.

2. (a) Short term (any one of):
       Heart rate increases. Breathing rate increases.
       Long term (any one of):
       Red blood cell production increases. Blood becomes thicker. Capillary density increases.
   (b) Increased breathing rate increases the rate at which new air is brought into the lungs (compensating for lower oxygen). Increased heart rate pumps blood more rapidly to tissues to improve oxygen delivery. Increased RBC production (and thicker blood) increases the level of hemoglobin that can be carried (increases oxygen-carrying capacity). Increased capillary density increases capacity for oxygen delivery to the tissues.

KEY TERMS: Mix and Match (page 213)

alveoli (sing. alveolus) (H), asthma (J), breathing (V), breathing rate (M), bronchi (O), bronchioles (Y), chronic bronchitis (K), emphysema (C), expiration (=exhalation) (I), gas exchange system (A), hemoglobin (S), inspiration (=inhalation) (X), intercostal muscles (E), intrapleural pressure (G), lungs (D), myoglobin (N), obstructive pulmonary disease (Z), oxygen-hemoglobin dissociation curve (W), pulmonary ventilation rate (PV) (U), residual volume (R), respiratory center (T), respiratory pigment (L), surfactant (E), tidal volume (B), trachea (Q), vital capacity (P).

© 2009-2013 **BIOZONE** International
ISBN: 978-1-927173-59-6
Photocopying Prohibited

The Human Diet (page 217)

1. Nutrients are required as (a) and (b) in any order:
   (a) An energy source
   (b) As the raw materials for metabolism, growth, and repair.

2. The new food pyramid distinguishes between "healthy" and "unhealthy" fats, and "healthy" and "unhealthy" (refined) carbohydrate sources. This is contrary to the older pyramid, which placed all fats together as to be avoided, and recommended that all carbohydrates form the base of the food pyramid. The new pyramid recommends a high intake of plant oils which correlates with reduced rates of heart disease.

3. Animal products provide a readily available, easily assimilated source of many nutrients, including B group vitamins and some fat soluble vitamins. Without animal products in the diet, vegans must plan carefully to ensure their nutritional needs are met though other sources. This usually means careful combining of food types to meet protein and vitamin/mineral requirements.

The Mouth and Pharynx (page 218)

1. (a) To break down the food by chewing.
   (b) To lubricate the food and mix it with saliva to being the process of chemical digestion.

2. The epiglottis prevents food from going into the trachea and instead directs it to the esophagus. This can be inferred from its position and by the fact that i is normally pointed upward during breathing but is more horizontal during swallowing.

3. Tonsils provide immune protection against pharyngeal and upper respiratory tract infections.

Moving Food Through the Digestive Tract (page 219)

1. (a) Peristalsis is the wave-like contractions of smooth muscle in the gut.
   (b) The outer longitudinal muscles contract ahead of the food, shortening and widening the tube so that it can receive the bolus. The inner circular muscles contract behind the bolus, pushing it forward into the widened space ahead.

2. (a) A sphincter is a valve of circular muscle that, by contraction, is able to close an orifice (opening).
   (b) Sphincters regulate the passage of food through the digestive tract and prevent food material moving the wrong way (reflex).

The Digestive Tract (page 220)

1. Structures as follows:

A	Mouth and teeth	G	Gall bladder
B	Salivary glands	H	Colon (or large intestine)
C	Esophagus	I	Small intestine
D	Liver	J	Rectum
E	Stomach	K	Appendix
F	Pancreas	L	Anus

   Region responsible for each function as follows:
   (a) I - small intestine   (e) F - pancreas (or B)
   (b) J - rectum   (f) D - liver
   (c) H - colon   (g) B - salivary gland
   (d) E - stomach

2. See diagram.

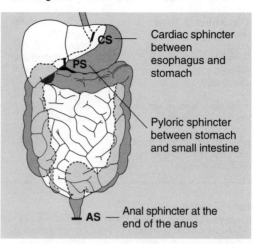

Cardiac sphincter between esophagus and stomach

Pyloric sphincter between stomach and small intestine

Anal sphincter at the end of the anus

3. (a) Lining (mucosa) of the stomach. Identified by gastric gland.
   (b) Lining (mucosa) of the small intestine. Identified by villi projecting into the lumen. Layer of muscle visible below connective tissue of villi.
   (c) Liver. Identified by the bile ducts.

4. (a) Stomach: A three layered muscular wall to produce the movements to mix the food into chyme. Rugae allow expansion of volume. Gastric glands specialized to produce acid, mucus, and pepsinogen (activated in acid to protein-digesting pepsin).
   (b) Small intestine: Fingerlike villi project into the lumen and provide large surface area for absorption of nutrients. Intestinal glands produce mucus to protect gut mucosa from damage and alkaline fluid to provide an appropriate pH for intestinal and pancreatic enzymes.
   (c) Large intestine: Simple columnar epithelium absorbs water from the slurry. Epithelium has tubular glands which produce mucus to lubricate colon walls and aid feces formation. Strong muscular walls move material through the colon.

5. (a) and (b): any two of the following in any order:
   Site: Stomach
   Enzyme: pepsin
   Purpose: Digestion of proteins to polypeptides

   Site: Pancreas
   Enzyme: pancreatic amylase
   Purpose: Digestion of starch to maltose.

   Site: Pancreas
   Enzymes: trypsin/chymotrypsin
   Purpose: Digestion of proteins to polypeptides.

   Site: Pancreas
   Enzyme: pancreatic lipase
   Purpose: Digestion of fats to fatty acids and glycerol.

   Site: Pancreas
   Enzymes: peptidases
   Purpose: Digestion of polypeptides to amino acids.

   Site: Intestinal mucosa
   Enzymes: peptidases.
   Purpose: Digestion of polypeptides to amino acids

   Site: Intestinal mucosa
   Enzymes: maltase, lactase, sucrase
   Purpose: Digestion of carbohydrates (maltose, lactose, sucrose respectively) into their components.

6. (a) The enzymes involved in digestion in different regions of the gut have specific pH optima (pH at which they operate most efficiently), so secretions are regionally pH appropriate. Note: For pepsin (stomach) this optimum is acid pH 1.5-2.0, for the enzymes in the small intestine, the optimum is alkaline pH 7.5-8.2.
   (b) The enzymes are secreted as inactive precursors in order to prevent their activity in the site of production and release (where they would damage the tissue). Once in the gut lumen, they can be activated to digest

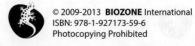
© 2009-2013 **BIOZONE** International
ISBN: 978-1-927173-59-6
Photocopying Prohibited

the food (the gut lining itself is protected by mucus).

7. (a) Food is moved through the gut by peristalsis (wave like contractions of smooth muscle).
   (b) Passage of food through the gut is regulated by sphincters, which allow material to pass more quickly through the gut or hold it back. Sphincter activity depends on speed of digestion, food type, hormones, and the fullness of the gut.
   Note: Sphincter contraction partly or completely closes an orifice.

8. (a) Passage too rapid: Too little water is reabsorbed leading to diarrhea.
   (b) Passage too slow: Too much water is reabsorbed leading to fecal compaction and constipation.

Absorption and Transport (page 223)

1. Question should read Describe the advantage of **villi and microvili** in the gut."
   Villi and microvilli increase the surface area for the absorption of nutrients into the underlying blood and lymphatic vessels. This increases the rate of food processing, enabling maximum gain from the food eaten.

1. (a) Active transport   (e) Active transport
   (b) Facilitated diffusion   (f) Diffusion
   (c) Active transport   (g) Diffusion
   (d) Active transport   (h) Diffusion

The Control of Digestion (page 224)

1. (a) Food in the mouth causes a reflex stimulation of salivary glands and stomach (parasympathetic stimulation via the vagus). The effect is a marked increase in salivary and gastric secretion.
   (b) Presence of fat and acid in the small intestine stimulates release of cholecystokinin and secretin from the intestinal mucosa. These hormones inhibit gastric motility and stimulate the secretions of the pancreas, the production and release of bile, and the secretions of the intestinal glands.
   (c) Stretching of the stomach stimulates the reflex secretion of the hormone gastrin from the gastric mucosa. Gastrin acts back on the stomach to increase gastric secretion and motility.

2. The vagus nerve provides the parasympathetic innervation of the gut, stimulating salivary, gastric, and pancreatic secretion.

3. Nervous and hormonal mechanisms are both involved in coordinating and regulating digestion. The autonomic nervous system controls salivation, and stimulation of the stomach and pancreas via the vagus nerve increases secretions of these organs. Hormones are released in response to chemical or nervous stimuli and act on digestive organs to regulate the release of digestive secretions.

The Liver (page 225)

1. Hepatocytes

2. Portal triad comprises bile ductule, branch of the hepatic portal vein, and branch of the hepatic portal artery.

3. (a) Vascular functions (one of):
   Manufactures heparin and blood proteins.
   Acts as a reservoir of blood, being able to store and release blood as required to maintain blood volume.
   (b) Metabolic functions (two of):
   Central to the metabolism of amino acids (e.g. deamination), fats (gluconeogenesis), and carbohydrates (e.g. glycogenolysis, glycogenesis).
   Synthesises cholesterol.
   Stores minerals and vitamins.
   Detoxifies poisons.
   (c) Digestive function: Secretes biles for the emulsification of fats.
   (d) Excretory functions (one of):
   Produces urea from amino acids for excretion of nitrogen

Excretes hormones
Metabolizes hemoglobin which is excreted in the bile.
   (e) Storage functions (one of):
   Stores blood
   Stores iron, copper, and vitamins (A, D, E, K, B_{12}).

The Histology of the Liver (page 226)

1. (a) **Supply 1**: Branches of the hepatic artery. **Purpose**: Supply of oxygen and nutrients to the liver tissue.
   (b) **Supply 2**: Hepatic portal vein. **Purpose**: Brings nutrient-rich blood to the liver for processing by the liver cells.

2. (a) **Bile canaliculi**: Carry the bile (secreted by the hepatocytes) to the bile ductules where it then flows into the bile duct.
   (b) **Phagocytic Kupffer cells**: Engulf microbes and break down spent red blood cells.
   (c) **Central vein**: Carries blood (mix of hepatic portal and arterial blood) that has passed through the liver lobule to the hepatic vein (which exits the liver).
   (d) **Sinusoids**: Blood spaces that carry the mix of hepatic portal and arterial blood through the lobules, for processing, and supply of oxygen and nutrients.

3. Venous supply through the hepatic portal system provides a supply of nutrient-rich blood from the gut directly to the liver for processing.

4. The liver is richly vascularised with a system of capillary-like sinusoids ramifying throughout. At any one time, more than half of the 10-20% of liver's volume is in the sinusoids.

5. Sinusoids are leakier than capillaries so small and medium sized proteins can easily leave and enter the blood.
   This facilitates exchanges between the blood and the hepatocytes.

Protein Metabolism in the Liver (page 227)

1. Aspects of protein metabolism (a-c in any order):
   (a) Transamination of amino acids to create new, non-essential amino acids.
   (b) Deamination of excess amino acids and production of urea in the urea cycle.
   (c) Synthesis of plasma proteins.

2. Deamination produces keto acids, which feed into the Krebs cycle and are oxidized to yield ATP, NH_2 joins with CO_2 and enters the orninthine cycle to produce urea.

3. Symptoms would be a build up of ammonia in the tissues and, unless addressed by management of diet to minimize protein content, it would be fatal.

Exercise, Fiber, and Gut Function (page 228)

1. (a) With a few exceptions, whole gut times overall were longest in the regime of rest and shortest in the run regime. The transition times for the ride regime were more variable but generally between the rest and run.
   (b) Exercise speeds the passage of food through the gut, probably through its effects on gut motility.

2. Insoluble dietary fiber increases the bulk of the stool, decreasing gut transit time and therefore increasing the frequency (and ease) of bowel movements. Soluble fiber helps to regulate lipid metabolism and blood sugar. Insoluble fiber in particular maintains a healthy gut by keeping gut transit times low and minimizing the problems caused by fecal compaction (implicated in cancers and other bowel problems such as hemorrhoids).

Malnutrition and Obesity (page 229)

1. (a) Obesity is regarded as a form of malnutrition because more food is consumed than is required to stay healthy. The food consumed is often highly processed and not nutritionally balanced, containing high levels of fat, sugar, and salt.
   (b) The two basic energy factors which determine how a persons weight will change are the energy consumed and the energy expended (exercise).

© 2009-2013 **BIOZONE** International
ISBN: 978-1-927173-59-6

2. (a) Overweight: 85.6-102.6 kg
   (b) Obese: over 102.6 kg

3. The calculation of BMI makes simplistic assumptions about the distribution of muscle and bone mass. It tends to overestimate "fatness" on those with more lean body mass (e.g. athletes or very muscular people) and underestimate "fatness" on those with less lean body mass (e.g. the elderly).

4. (a) Percentage of obese people is lower (up to 50% lower among women) in people with incomes that place them 400% above the poverty line and increases progressively with reduction in income.
   (b) Highly educated people will (for the most part) have higher paying jobs than a person with little education. They are able to spend more money on healthy food (fruit, vegetables, lean cuts of meat). They may also know more about the importance of eating a balanced diet to obtain good nutrition, so make better food choices.
   (c) A high proportion of people in developing nations live at or below the poverty line and their access to food choices is limited, especially when the foods that are cheapest tend to be those that are nutritionally poor (refined CHO.

5. The root cause of obesity - eating too many calories for energy needs - is often coincident with the consumption of a highly processed (high carbohydrate, high fat) diet. Such diets are poor in vitamins, minerals, and fibre and, even when eaten in excess, provide inadequate nutrition, especially for high needs groups such as young children.

Deficiency Diseases (page 231)

1. A deficiency disease refers to any disease caused by a lack of an essential nutrient, such as a vitamin or a mineral.

2. Young children, pregnant women, and athletes have higher than normal energy requirements and some quite specific vitamin and mineral requirements. It is more difficult for these particular groups to satisfy their energy and nutrient requirements through normal eating. **Extra information:** Children are generally very active and are growing rapidly, so they have a high requirement for both energy and minerals such as iron and calcium. Athletes have high energy demands because of their increased physical activity and higher rates of tissue repair. Their need for some minerals, such as iron, is also higher than for non-active adults. Pregnant women have slightly higher energy needs than non-pregnant women, as well as specific nutrient requirements (e.g. for iron and folate) associated with nourishing a developing foetus. Children, with their smaller capacity, must eat more frequently. Athletes must eat more, particularly of energy and nutrient dense foods. Pregnant women should take care to avoid alcohol, and make food choices that supply their increased nutrient demands with only a moderate increase in calorie intake.

3. (a) Iron is required for the production of hemoglobin and a lack of iron in the diet results in lower than normal levels of hemoglobin in red blood cells. Less oxygen will be able to be transported around the body and this results in breathlessness and fatigue (the typical symptoms of anemia).
   (b) Women of child-baring age, who are not pregnant, menstruate regularly and, for some, blood losses can be heavy. This is often coupled with a lower overall food intake and a lower intake of red meat, making women more susceptible to iron deficient anemia.

4. Dietary supplementation can be achieved by adding the vitamin or mineral to a regularly used food product (e.g. folic acid and iron to breads and cereals, and iodine to table salt). The benefits of dietary supplementation in this way stem from reaching a large sector of the general population easily in order to provide an essential element that may be deficient in the diet and contributes a lot to public health. In the case of iodine, which is widely deficient in soils and therefore also in food, supplementation is a public health exercise, which prevents goiter in the population (particularly poorer sectors who cannot afford to buy supplements).

5. A zinc deficiency results in impaired muscle function because zinc is required for both enzyme activity and gene expression. Zinc is also important in sexual development, e.g. in the production of sperm, and a deficiency of zinc results in a delay in puberty.

6. Alcohol damages the cells lining the small intestine and inhibits fat absorption so, even if dietary intake is adequate, many fat soluble vitamins will not be absorbed or utilized properly.

Infection and Gut Function (page 233)

1. The bacterium *Vibrio cholerae*.

2. If untreated, the copious diarrhea can quickly lead to severe dehydration and a consequent collapse of all body systems (particularly kidney and heart failure).

3. Treatment with ORS provides replaces the electrolytes lost with the diarrhea as well as the water. Glucose or sucrose in the ORS enhance electrolytes absorption. Drinking water alone does not address electrolyte loss.

4. (a) By causing osmotic withdrawal of water into the intestine.
   (b) Sugars are required for the cotransport of sodium into the intestinal epithelial cells.
   (c) The patient might stop treatment and this would delay or prevent recovery.

5. ORS deliver high concentrations of glucose and sodium ions to the gut lumen where they are transported into the epithelial cells by the sodium-glucose pump. Chloride ions follow the Na^+ into the cell, and then water follows down its osmotic gradient into the cell. Water can then enter the blood by osmosis to restore blood volume.
   Extra note: Glucose also leaves the epithelial cell and enters the bloodstream, but this is taken away and metabolized. Also note that the glucose transporter on the basal plasma membrane of the epithelial cell enables glucose to enter the interstitial space and then the blood by facilitated diffusion, unlike the glucose cotransporter which takes up glucose from the gut lumen into the cell.

6. Water and ion fluxes in response to cholera infection need to be understood to deliver an appropriate treatment. The first step is knowing that the cholera toxin affects chloride transport so that chloride ions enter the gut lumen at a higher rate than normal. Knowing that sodium ions and then water will follow reveals the cause of the diarrhea. A treatment that increases epithelial cell uptake of sodium and chloride to counteract these losses can then be devised.

7. The cholera toxin passes through the plasma membrane of the intestinal epithelial cell and acts as a signalling molecule, activating pathways that produce cyclic AMP from ATP. The cAMP opens the CFTR channels causing chloride ions to leave the cell and enter the gut lumen. Sodium ions follow the electrochemical gradient and water follows down its osmotic gradient, so salt (NaCl) and water leave the gut in copious amounts.

8. As with any trials, there is a risk that a new product may worsen the diarrhea or have unexpected undesirable side effects. If a new product is ineffectual, there is a risk that the inadequacy of the treatment could be life threatening. The ethics of trials are especially fraught when the trials involve one group of patients receiving a placebo (no effect) or a less effective treatment (these are used to measure the extent to which the new product is better.

KEY TERMS: Mix and Match (page 235)

1. absorption (L), anus (M), assimilation (T), diet (K), digestion (Y), digestive enzymes (P), digestive system (W), egestion (E), esophagus (A), exocrine (F), feces (O), gall bladder (V), ingestion (X), intestinal villus (I), large intestine (AA), liver (C), malnutrition (BB), mouth (B), oral rehydration solution (Z), pancreas (G), peristalsis (D), pharynx (S), saliva (H), small intestine (R), stomach (N), swallowing (J), tooth (U), type 2 diabetes mellitus (Q).

Waste Products in Humans (page 239)

1. **Carbon dioxide**: <u>Origin</u>: All metabolizing cells.
<u>Organ of excretion</u>: Lungs.
Water: <u>Origin</u>: All metabolizing cells.
<u>Organs of excretion</u>: Lungs, kidneys, gut, skin.
Bile pigments: <u>Origin</u>: Breakdown of hemoglobin in liver.
<u>Organ of excretion</u>: Gut. The breakdown product passes out in the feces.
Urea: <u>Origin</u>: Produced in the liver from ammonia (resulting after breakdown of amino and nucleic acids). <u>Organs of excretion</u>: Kidneys, skin.
Ions: <u>Origin</u>: General result of cellular metabolism. <u>Organs of excretion</u>: Kidneys, skin, gut.
Hormones: <u>Origin</u>: Endocrine organs, sometimes ingested (synthetic hormones and anti-inflammatories). <u>Organs of excretion</u>: Kidneys, skin.
Poisons: <u>Origin</u>: Ingested or inhaled from external sources. <u>Organs of excretion</u>: Kidneys.
Drugs: <u>Origin</u>: Ingested or inhaled from external sources. <u>Organs of excretion</u>: Kidneys.

2. The liver produces urea from ammonia (urea cycle) and bile pigments from the breakdown of hemoglobin.

3. A hormone (human chorionic gonadotropin or HCG) produced in excess during establishment of pregnancy.

4. – Problems of fluid retention: edema and retention of fluids containing toxins and waste products.
   – Problems of salt retention leading to hypertension and heart problems as the heart works harder to move the blood through constricted vessels.
   – Problems with the retention of ions other than sodium leading to the toxic effects of high ion levels.
   – Poisoning of the body with its own metabolic wastes eventually leads to coma and death.

Water Budget in Humans (page 240)

1. Metabolism involves the oxidation of glucose to produce ATP. A by-product of this process is water ($6O_2 + C_6H_{12}O_6 \rightarrow 6CO_2 + 6H_2O$)

2. (a) Intestinal infection resulting in diarrhea.
   (b) Inadequate access to fluids.
   (c) Excessive vomiting.
   (d) Excessive sweating.

3. Excessive water intake, without associated intake of electrolytes, has a diluting effect where there is an increase in total body water relative to the total amount of exchangeable sodium. This causes an osmotic shift of water from the plasma into the cells, particularly the brain cells. Typical symptoms include nausea, vomiting, headache and malaise. **Note**: As the hyponatremia worsens, confusion, diminished reflexes, convulsions, stupor or coma may occur. Nausea is, itself, a stimulus for the release of ADH, which promotes the retention of water, leading to a positive feedback loop and the potential for a vicious cycle of hyponatremia and its symptoms.

The Urinary System (page 241)

1. (a) Kidney: produces urine and regulates blood volume.
   (b) Ureters: convey urine to the bladder
   (c) Bladder: stores urine
   (d) Urethra: conveys urine to the outside
   (e) Renal artery: carries blood from aorta to kidney. Supplies the kidney with oxygenated blood.
   (f) Renal vein: carries blood from kidney to vena cava. Returns blood from the kidney to the venous circulation.
   (g) Renal capsule: covers the kidney and protects it against trauma and infection.

2. 99.4%

3. (a) A nephron is the selective filtering element in the kidney. It is the functional unit of the kidney.
   (b) The nephron produces a filtrate from the blood, modifies the filtrate and produces the final excretory fluid (called urine).

4. (a) Transitional epithelium is found in the bladder.

   (b) It means the walls of the bladder can be stretched without the outer cells breaking apart from one another.

5. The sphincter allows the voluntary voiding of urine (urination or micturition).

The Physiology of the Kidney (page 243)

1. The high blood pressure is needed for ultrafiltration, i.e. to force small molecules such as water, glucose, amino acids, sodium chloride and urea through the capillaries of the glomerulus and the basement membrane and epithelium of Bowman's capsule.

2. (a) Glomerular filtration: Produces an initial filtrate of the blood that is similar in composition to blood and can be modified to produce the final urine.
   (b) Active secretion: Secretion allows the body to get rid of unwanted substances into the urine.
      Explanatory detail: Active secretion of chloride in the ascending limb (with sodium following passively) contributes to the maintenance of the salt gradient in the extracellular fluid (this gradient allows water to be reabsorbed in the collecting duct). Secretion of toxins and unwanted ions into the filtrate in the distal tubules allows the blood composition to be adjusted and poisons to be excreted. Energy is used to secrete these substances against their concentration gradients
   (c) Reabsorption: Essential process that allows the useful substances (required by the body) to be retained from the filtrate (particularly the initial filtrate, where 90% is reabsorbed). The body would waste energy if these substances were not retained.
   (d) Osmosis: Osmotic loss of water allows the urine to be concentrated (via loss of water).
      Explanatory detail: Osmosis is important in two regions of the nephron: In the descending limb of the loop of Henle, osmotic loss of water concentrates the filtrate so that salt can be withdrawn from the ascending limb to contribute to the salt gradient in the extracellular fluid. In the collecting duct, loss of water by osmosis provides the final concentration of the urine

3. (a) The salt gradient allows water to be withdrawn from the urine (allows the urine to be concentrated). **Explanatory detail**: Because the salt gradient increases through the medulla, the osmotic gradient is maintained and water can be continually withdrawn from the urine.
   (b) Salt gradient is produced by the active and passive movement of salt from the filtrate into the extracellular fluid in the medulla.

Control of Urine Output (page 245)

1. (a) Diabetes insipidus is characterized by excretion of large amounts of very dilute urine (accompanied by a great thirst). Lack of ADH causes excessive urine production (ADH reduces urine output).
   (b) Diabetes insipidus is treated by administering antidiuretic hormone (ADH) by injection.

2. Alcohol inhibits ADH release causing greater urine output, resulting in dehydration and thirst.

3. Decreases or increases in blood volume are detected by hypothalamic osmoreceptors and the secretion of ADH increases or decreases accordingly. This results in an adjustment of urine output until homeostasis is restored. The adjustments made in response to the ADH release act back on the hypothalamus to counter further change. Note that, by a more complex mechanism, low blood volumes also stimulate the release of aldosterone, which induces Na^+ reabsorption in the kidney and (by osmosis) more absorption of water and thus restoration of blood volume.

4. Active transport of sodium and chloride in the nephron is used to establish and maintain the salt gradient through the kidney that is essential to its ability to produce a concentrated urine. When salt transport is inhibited, the ability to concentrate the urine is also impaired and urine volume increases as a result.

© 2009-2013 **BIOZONE** International
ISBN: 978-1-927173-59-6
Photocopying Prohibited

Urine Analysis (page 246)

1. Urinalysis is quick and simple to perform and there are diagnostic parameters for particular metabolites. This makes diagnosis and treatment potentially very quick and cost-effective.

2. Urine is voided and its role is to rid the body of nitrogenous wastes and excess ions. Depending on diet etc, urine pH can vary quite widely, as the kidneys adjust the composition of the blood. In contrast, the pH of blood can not vary to the same extent. It must continuously circulate and the efficiency of metabolic processes depends on it staying within narrow limits.

3. (a) Red blood cells in the urine (hematouria) and therefore bleeding in the urinogenital tract.
   (b) Infection in the urinogenital tract.

4. Athletes withhold drug use for a period before testing so that the body has had time to break down and metabolize the drug and excrete it (thereby avoiding detection).

Fluid and Electrolyte Balance (page 247)

1. The intracellular fluid compartment is the fluid found within the body's cells. it accounts for 60-65% of the body's water and is important for the metabolic reactions occurring within their fluid environment. The extracellular fluid compartments (the fluid within and outside vessels) make up the remainder of the body's water and are important for bathing the cells, maintaining the integrity of hollow structures (like blood and lymph vessels) and providing the environment for the necessary exchanges between the extracellular and intracellular compartments.

2. (a) Fall in blood volume caused by blood loss (as a result of trauma) or a sudden loss of blood pressure (e.g. as a result of shock) or a drop in electrolyte levels.
   (b) A drop in blood volume is detected by the juxtaglomerular cells of the kidney which monitor the blood in the afferent arteriole of the glomerulus. They respond by producing the enzyme renin, which catalyzes the formation of angiotensin II in the blood. It is angiotensin II that causes blood vessels to constrict (which raises blood pressure) and stimulates the adrenal cortex to release aldosterone (which causes tubular reabsorption of sodium and water by osmosis). Angiotensin II also stimulates the thirst center of the hypothalamus to promote drinking. When blood volume increases, the juxtaglomerular cells cease to be stimulated and renin production falls.

Acid-Base Balance (page 248)

1. Blood is continuously circulating and carrying with it the products of metabolic activity (which are generally acidic and could potentially alter pH considerably if the blood were not buffered). The efficiency (and continuation) of metabolic processes depends on blood pH staying within the narrow range required by the enzymes catalyzing metabolic processes.

2. Metabolic acidosis is caused by increased production of H^+ by the body or the inability of the body to form bicarbonate (HCO_3^-) in the kidney. Causes can be varied by include diarrhea (loss of HCO_3^-), renal failure, starvation, and poisoning.

3. (a) Chemical buffers in the blood tie up excess H^+ or bases temporarily. The bicarbonate ion and its acid (carbonic acid) are in a dynamic equilibrium to mop up excess H^+ and OH^-. The system is supported by the charged groups on blood proteins, which act as H^+ acceptors or donors.
   (b) If a base is added to the system, the OH^- is neutralized to a weak base (HCO_3^-)

4. (a) The respiratory response to excess H^+ is an increase in the rate and depth of breathing.
   (b) The excess H^+ comes from the dissociation of carbonic acid (H_2CO_3), which arises as a result of carbon dioxide combining with water.
   (c) Respiratory acidosis is the result of decreased

ventilation of the pulmonary alveoli. This can arise as a result of airway obstruction (e.g. asthma), depression of the respiratory center (e.g. as a result of trauma), certain diseases (e.g. muscular dystrophy), and obesity.

5. It is only through the renal system that excess acids and bases can be permanently eliminated from the body. The main ways this is achieved is by excretion of hydrogen ions and reabsorption of hydroxide ions (since most metabolic wastes are acidic).

Kidney Dialysis (page 249)

1. The dialyzing solution is constantly replaced because it needs to be free of urea and other wastes in order to maintain the concentration gradient between the blood and the dialyzate. Without a gradient, urea and other wastes would remain in the blood.

2. Other ions and small molecules do not diffuse into the dialyzate because they are at a similar concentration in both blood and dialyzate, i.e. the dialyzate has a similar ionic composition to blood and there is no concentration gradient for these molecules.

3. The urea passes into the dialyzate because there is always less urea present in dialyzate than in blood. Therefore there is a concentration gradient for urea between the blood and the dialyzate.

4. The general transport process involved in dialysis is diffusion; the movement of molecules from a region of high concentration to a region of low concentration.

5. The dialyzing solution runs in the opposite direction to that of the blood (similar to countercurrent heat exchangers) because in this way almost all of the urea can be removed from the blood in the shortest possible time. **Further explanation:** The blood at the beginning of the dialysis column (high urea) encounters dialyzate that already contains some urea, but there is still a concentration gradient from blood to dialyzate. By the time the blood reaches the end of the dialysis column most of the urea has been removed, but it encounters fresh dialyzing solution (no urea) and there is still a concentration gradient. Having blood and dialyzate running in opposite direction maintains the concentration gradient for a longer time. If the two fluids ran in the same direction the concentrations would quickly equilibrate, and urea would cease to pass into the dialyzate.

6. The clot and bubble trap are necessary in order to remove small blood coagulations (clotting) and air bubbles which might form during the dialysis process. If these were allowed to enter the bloodstream they could cause stroke or embolism (blood vessel obstruction).

Kidney Transplants (page 250)

1. Acute renal failure arises suddenly as a result of infection, blood loss, or dehydration. ARF is characterized by a very sudden drop in urine volume. Chronic renal failure develops over months or years as a result of poorly controlled diabetes or high blood pressure, or chronic kidney disase. Unlike ARF, recovery from CRF is not possible.

2. (a) Creatinine is produced at a relatively constant rate and is usually filtered out by the kidneys, so if the levels increase in the blood it would indicate that the kidneys are not operating normally.
   (b) Creatinine clearance is a better measure of renal function than serum creatinine because it indicates early if kidneys are failing. Serum creatinine levels will only rise when kidney function is already impaired.

3. Kidney transplants (if the tissue is a good match) offer a high chance of success and a normal life away from the constraints of continual dialysis. Problems include the need to take immunosuppressant drugs and the risk that a suitable donor will not be available when required. Lifetime dialysis is expensive, time consuming and cannot help regulate blood pressure in the way that a kidney can. There is also a risk of infection (higher with peritoneal dialysis).

© 2009-2013 **BIOZONE** International
ISBN: 978-1-927173-59-6
Photocopying Prohibited

KEY TERMS: Mix and Match (page 251)

aldosterone (Q), antidiuretic hormone (ADH) (I), bladder (S), Bowman's capsule (V), collecting duct (G), cortex (of kidney) (N), distal convoluted tubule (O), electrolyte (M), excretion (P), extracellular fluid (D), glomerulus (X), intracellular fluid (H), kidney (U), loop of Henle (E), medulla (of kidney) (R), micturition (= urination) (F), nephron (A), osmoreceptors (J), proximal convoluted tubule (B) renal corpuscle (T), renal dialysis (AA), renal failure (Z), renal pelvis (L), ultrafiltration (C), urethra (K), ureter (W), urine (Y).

Gametes (page 255)

1. Once deposited in the vagina, sperm must be able to move through the uterus and into the oviducts to reach and fertilize the ovum. Sperm only live for about 48 hours, so they must be able to move quickly to reach the ovum to attempt fertilization before they die.

2. (a) Ova move as a result of the wave-like motion of the cilia in the Fallopian tube.
   (b) Ova must be larger than sperm because they must contain nutritional resources to support the early development of the embryo.

3. (a) Acrosome: its enzymes break down the outer membrane of the ovum so that the haploid nucleus of the sperm cell can enter.
   (b) Nucleus: contains the male haploid genes that join with the female equivalent to produce the diploid zygote.
   (c) Mitochondria: supply the energy (as ATP) needed for sperm motility (swimming to the ovum).
   (d) Flagellum: provides the propulsion for the sperm cell to swim to the ovum.

Male Reproductive System (page 256)

1. (a) Vas deferens   (e) Epididymis
   (b) Bladder   (f) Urethra
   (c) Seminal vesicle   (g) Testis
   (d) Prostate gland   (h) Scrotal sac (scrotum)

2. (a) Conducts sperm to the urethra.
   (b) Stores urine.
   (c) Produces secretions that add to the semen.
   (d) Produces secretions that forms part of the semen.
   (e) Coiled tube where sperm mature
   (f) Conducts sperm and urine to the outside.
   (g) Produces sperm and testosterone (male hormone).
   (h) Holds the testes (outside the body at the cooler temperature required for sperm production).

3. (1) Testosterone is needed for development of the primary sexual characteristics in males (genitalia). (2) At puberty, testosterone causes the secondary sexual characteristics to develop (sperm, body hair, muscle growth, deepening of voice). (3) In adults it maintains sex drive and production of sperm.

4. Main roles of the male reproductive system is to produce sperm and deliver it to the female.

Spermatogenesis (page 257)

1. (a) Spermatogenesis
   (b) Testis
   (c) Four
   (d) Meiosis

2. LH stimulates synthesis and secretion of testosterone which is required for sperm production. FSH supports the Sertoli cells and sperm maturation.

3. About 100-400 million sperm are needed because only a very small percentage of them eventually reach the ovum (remember that the sperm must negotiate the cervix and then find their way into the fallopian tube). **Extra note**: Although only one sperm is needed to fertilize the egg, the combined action of the enzymes from a large number of sperm is needed to help digest the jelly-like barrier around the egg.

Female Reproductive System (page 258)

1. (a) Uterus   (d) Cervix
   (b) Fallopian tube (oviduct)   (e) Vagina
   (c) Ovary   (f) Clitoris

2. (a) Houses developing embryo, establishes placenta.
   (b) The usual place of fertilization and also conducts the egg to the uterus.
   (c) Produces ova (eggs) and female reproductive hormones (estrogen and progesterone).
   (d) Entry to uterus. Its mucus protects the uterus from invasion by microorganisms. It is a powerful muscle that prevents the loss of the fetus in pregnancy.
   (e) Birth canal. Receives penis in sexual intercourse, pathway for delivery of the baby at term during labor.

3. (a) A = Ovary.
   (b) Ovulation.
   (c) Oogenesis (gametogenesis is also correct).

4. Fertilization occurs in the Fallopian tube (oviduct).

The Menstrual Cycle (page 259)

1. (a) FSH
   (b) LH

2. (a) Estrogen.
   (b) Promotes repair and growth of the uterine lining.
   (c) The follicles are reabsorbed.

3. (a) Progesterone (estrogen in smaller amounts).
   (b) Promotes full development of the uterine lining (endometrium). If fertilization occurs, progesterone maintains the thickened endometrium and acts to prevent further follicle development.

4. Menstruation triggered by a sharp drop in progesterone levels following degeneration of the corpus luteum.

Oogenesis (page 260)

1. (a) Oogenesis
   (b) In the ovarian follicle within the ovary

2. Sperm are continually produced within the testes from puberty onwards. One spermatogonium produces four identical mature sperm. Many millions of sperm are produced every day. In contrast, a female is born with her full complement of eggs, which develop in stages. One egg matures and is released at every menstrual cycle until menopause. Only one mature ovum is produced from an oogonium.

3. Males continue to produce new sperm throughout their reproductive life span. Because the sperm are newly produced, a higher proportion are genetically viable and healthy. Females are born with their full complement of immature eggs. As a female ages so do the eggs, so egg viability (therefore fertility) declines with age. Oogenesis eventually ceases at menopause.

Control of the Menstrual Cycle (page 261)

1. See table at the top of the next page.

2. In general principle, the product of a series of (hormone controlled) reactions controls its own production by turning off the pathway when it reaches a certain level. Each stage in the cycle is precisely controlled by the interplay of various hormones and the negative feedback effect that they have on their controlling factors (hormones). **Exemplar**: *e.g. one hormone (e.g. estrogen) is produced as a result of the activity of another hormone (e.g. FSH). At a certain level, the estrogen inhibits further FSH release so that the further development of follicles is prevented. Estrogen levels then fall and the next stage in the cycle can proceed.*

3. In males FSH and LH (called ICSH in males) regulate spermatogenesis (sperm production). Note that ICSH operates through stimulating testosterone secretion.

Hormone	Main site of secretion	Main effects and site of action during the menstrual cycle
GnRH	Hypothalamus	Stimulates anterior pituitary to secrete LH and FSH.
FSH	Anterior pituitary	Stimulates the growth of ovarian follicles.
LH	Anterior pituitary	Stimulates ovulation and development of corpus luteum.
Estrogens	Graafian follicle	At high level, stimulates LH surge. Promotes growth and repair of uterine lining.
Progesterone	Corpus luteum	Maintains endometrium. Inhibits FSH/LH. Sharp drop triggers menstruation.

The Placenta (page 262)

1. A double layered, spongy, vascular tissue, formed from both fetal and maternal tissues in the wall of the uterus. The fetal portion of the placenta sends fingerlike projections (villi) into the maternal endometrium. These villi contain the capillaries that connect the fetal arteries and vein. The blood vessels of the mother and fetus are in close proximity, forming a complex network that allows for the exchange of nutrients, respiratory gases, wastes.

2. (a) Fetal arteries: Deoxygenated and containing nitrogenous wastes.
   (b) Fetal vein: Oxygenated and containing nutrients.

3. (a) They cross the placenta and are taken up by the fetus. The fetus does not have the capacity to filter out toxins. Any substance capable of diffusing into the fetal capillaries does so.
   (b) CO diffuses across the placenta into the fetal capillaries and occupies the fetal hemoglobin, reducing the oxygen carrying capacity of fetal blood and causing oxygen deprivation.

Fertilization and Early Growth (page 263)

1. (a) **Capacitation**: Changes in the surface of the sperm cell (caused by the acid environment of the vagina) that make possible its adhesion to the oocyte.
   (b) **Acrosome reaction**: The release of enzymes from the acrosome at the head of the sperm. These enzymes digest a pathway through the follicle cells and the zona pellucida.
   (c) **Fusion** of the egg and sperm membranes: Enables the sperm nucleus to enter the egg. The fusion causes a sudden depolarization of the membrane that forms a fast block to further sperm entry.
   (d) **Cortical reaction**: A permanent change in the egg surface that provides a slow (permanent) block to sperm entry. Involves the release of cortical granules into the perivitelline space, followed by the release of substances from the granules that raise and harden the vitelline layer.
   (e) **Fusion** of egg and sperm nuclei: Results in the formation of a diploid zygote and initiates the rapid cell division that follows fertilization.

2. It is necessary to prevent fertilization of the egg by more than one sperm because this would result in too many chromosomes in the zygote (making the zygote non-viable or unable to survive). Triploidy (a condition resulting from two sperm fertilizing an egg) is frequently found among spontaneous miscarriages.

3. (a) Oocyte is arrested in metaphase of meiosis II after it has already undergone the first meiotic division.
   (b) Meiotic division proceeds to completion if the egg is fertilized (i.e. fertilization triggers completion).

4. (a) Zygote nucleus: sperm: 50%, egg: 50%
   (b) Zygote cytoplasm: sperm: 0%, egg: 100%

5. Cleavage is the rapid early cell division of the fertilized egg to produce the ball of cells that will become the blastocyst. Cleavage increases the number of cells but not the size of the zygote.

6. (a) Implantation (of blastocyst) is important to establish the close contact between the developing fetus and the uterine lining. The uterine lining can then provide for the early nourishment of the embryo.
   (b) Chorion and the allantois.
   (c) The amniotic sac is filled with fluid and so provides shock absorption for the embryo, cushioning it against damage.
   (d) Early development of the heart and blood vessels is essential for establishing blood flow around the developing fetus, as well as to and from the placenta (the source of nourishment and waste disposal for the fetus for most of its development).

7. This the period during which most organ development occurs and the developing tissues are most prone to damage from drugs.

Apoptosis and Development (page 265)

1. Syndactyly arises when the rate of apoptosis in the developing limb has been too low to remove the tissue between the digits before the close of the developmental sequence (hence the lack of differentiation between the two toes, which remain partly joined).

2. Any one of the reasons from the following explanation:
   - Apoptosis is a carefully regulated process, which occurs in response to particular signalling factors. Necrosis is the result of traumatic damage.
   - Apoptosis results in membrane-bound cell fragments whereas necrosis results in lyzsing and spillage of cell contents.
   - Apoptosis results in cell shrinkage and contraction of the chromatin, which does not occur in necrosis.

3. Roles of apoptosis, (a) and (b) any two of the following in any order:
   - Resorption of the larval tail during amphibian metamorphosis.
   - Sloughing of the endometrium in menstruation.
   - The formation of the correct connections (synapses) between neurons in the brain (surplus cells must be eliminated by apoptosis).
   - Controlled removal of virus-infected cells.
   - Controlled removal of cancerous cells.

The Hormones of Pregnancy (page 266)

1. (a) The placenta does not develop fully until three months or so into the pregnancy. Before this, the progesterone to maintain the endometrium must come from the corpus luteum.
   (b) Progesterone and estrogens.

2. (a) Estrogen (high levels) and oxytocin.
   (b) Any two of:
      • Declining progesterone levels.
      • Loss of placental competency (placenta deteriorates).
      • High estrogen levels increasing uterine sensitivity to oxytocin.
      • Peak in oxytocin.
      • The physiological state of the fetus (e.g. level of stress hormones).

 © 2009-2013 **BIOZONE** International
ISBN: 978-1-927173-59-6
Photocopying Prohibited

Birth and Lactation (page 267)

1. (a) Stage 1: **Dilation**: The time during which the cervix is dilating (opening).
   (b) Stage 2: **Expulsion**: The time between full dilation and delivery during which the baby is pushed to the vaginal entrance, the head crowns, and the baby is pushed out.
   (c) Stage 3: **Placental stage**: The delivery (passing out) of the placenta. The placental blood vessels constrict to stop bleeding.

2. (a) Estrogen
   (b) Prostaglandins, factors released from the placenta (as its function becomes compromised towards the end of pregnancy), and the physiological state of the baby itself.

3. The umbilical cord continues to function (supplying oxygen) until the baby is breathing on its own.

4. (a) Hormone: Oxytocin. Production: posterior pituitary.
   (b) Hormone: Prolactin. Production: anterior pituitary.
   (c) Hormone: Oxytocin. Production: posterior pituitary.

5. Progesterone inhibits prolactin secretion.

6. (a) and (b) any two of the following:
   - It helps to form early, close contact between the mother and infant (bonding).
   - Breast fed babies do not get too fat.
   - The infant has better control over its own milk intake (said to prevent overeating in later life).
   - Fats and iron from breast milk are better absorbed than those in cow's and the milk is easier to digest.
   - The sodium (salt) content of human milk is lower than cow's milk and more suited to infants needs.
   - Breast feeding provides important antibodies that help prevent gut problems and improve immunity to respiratory infections and meningitis.
   - The act of sucking on the breast promotes development of the jaw, facial muscles, and teeth (sucking from a bottle requires much less effort).
   - There is less likely to be an allergic reaction to a mothers milk than to cow's milk or to a formula.
   - Breastfeeding helps the mother's reproductive organs return to a normal state more rapidly.
   - While it continues, breastfeeding reduces the likelihood of another pregnancy.

7. (a) Colostrum is very high in maternal antibodies and has very little sugar and virtually no fat. Milk formed later has a higher fat content.
   (b) It is essential that the baby's system be provided with a good supply of antibodies in preparation for its early days outside the uterus. The composition of colostrum also assists in the adjustment of the infant gut to food.

8. Nutritional composition changes because the baby's nutritional requirements (e.g. for protein and fat) change as its grows.

9. The breast feeding mother should feed more frequently (on demand as the infant becomes hungrier) and this will induce greater milk production.

Contraception (page 269)

1. **Combined oral contraceptive** pills utilize the normal negative feedback mechanisms operating in the menstrual cycle. By providing an artificially high level of reproductive hormones (estrogen and progesterone), they prevent release of the pituitary hormones (FSH and LH) that induce follicle development and ovulation.

2. OCPs suppress follicle development and ovulation whereas the mini-pill does not affect the normal cycle of egg production and release; it merely thickens cervical mucus and prevents sperm entry, and prevents endometrial thickening.

3. OCPs offer effective contraception because they work either by preventing ovulation, or by providing an effective natural barrier to sperm entry at the cervix. Used properly, the chance of fertilization is almost nil.

Diseases of the Reproductive System (page 270)

1. Early detection of cancer allows the cancerous tissue to be treated (by radiation, chemotherapy, or surgical removal) before it spreads (metastasizes) to other parts of the body.

2. Ovarian and prostate cancer are more likely to kill because they are largely asymptomatic (or the symptoms are undetected) for a long time. This gives time for the cancer to spread to other parts of the body (and makes it more difficult to treat).

Treating Female Infertility (page 271)

1. (a) Drugs may induce release of FSH from the pituitary so that development of ova is stimulated.
   (b) Some drugs contain FSH and/or LH and directly induce the development and release of many ova.

2. (a) Where the fallopian tubes are blocked.
   (b) Where the ovaries are not functioning normally (a donor egg may be necessary).

3. Risk associated with fertility drugs:
   Multiple pregnancy (twins or triplets). These involve a higher risk of early miscarriage, pregnancy problems, and premature birth.

In Vitro Fertilization (page 272)

1. Any three of:
   - Failure to achieve or maintain and erection.
   - Abnormal ejaculation.
   - Low sperm production.
   - Poor sperm motility.
   - Poor sperm survival.
   - Vas deferens blocked or deformed.

2. Any three of:
   - Fallopian tubes blocked, damaged, or absent.
   - Problems with ovulation (failure of eggs to mature or be released).
   - Abnormality or disorder of the uterus that prevents implantation or growth of the embryo.
   - Cervical mucus forms antibodies to the sperm.

3. **IVF**: The **female is given hormones** to stimulate the release of several eggs. The **eggs are then removed** using a suction device and laparoscopy. The **eggs are mixed with sperm** outside the body. Once fertilization has occurred the **egg is cultured** to the 8- or 16-cell (blastocyst) stage. It is **then placed in the uterus** for implantation and further growth.

4. Student's own response based on their own opinions, research, and ethical stance.

Growth and Development (page 274)

1. The size of the skull becomes proportionately much smaller as an infant grows (birth to adulthood).

2. In the first period of rapid growth the face continues to grow outwards, reducing the relative proportions of the cranium, and the limbs elongate as a result of increasing ossification of cartilage. In the period up to two years, infants also develop so that they can hold their head up, sit up, crawl, and then walk.

3. The second period of rapid growth occurs at puberty in response to the rapid increase in secretion of sex steroids and growth hormone. Each gender develops their secondary sexual characteristics and there is a second increase in height.

4. (a) Growth velocity drops rapidly in the first two years of life (although their absolute growth remains rapid).
   (b) The graph infers that the rate of growth before birth is very high.
   (c) Between 12 and 14 years

5. As an infant becomes physically more capable, it develops the gross and fine motor skills to perform increasingly more advanced tasks. The infant begins to manipulate objects, talk, move with purpose, and play (with the objective of play

being to further develop cognitive skills).

Sexual Development (page 275)

1. **Primary** sexual characteristics are the distinguishing characteristics that are either male or female (i.e. penis and testes, or vagina, uterus, and ovaries). **Secondary** sexual characteristics are male or female characteristics that develop after puberty under the influence of reproductive hormones, e.g. facial and pubic hair, breast development, deposition of fat and muscle.

2. Testosterone.

3. Development of heavier musculature, increased body and facial hair, deepening of voice.

4. (a) Fat deposits serve as an energy reserve for the maintenance of pregnancy.
    (b) The menstrual cycle may stop and with it ovulation. This results in (usually temporary) infertility.

5. (a) Corpus luteum, placenta (in pregnancy).
    (b) Preparation of the uterus to receive a fertilized egg, maintenance of pregnancy (especially through maintenance of the placenta), inhibition of gonadotropins so that no further follicles develop.

Aging (page 276)

1. Aging is caused by cells dying and not being replaced or being replaced at a slower rate than early in life. These changes result in observable deterioration of tissues, such as skin and muscle (cell renewal rates are lower than the rate at which cells die).

2. (a) Muscle fibers maximum: 15-25.
    (b) half fibers are lost by age 80.
    (c) No

3. Main effect is decline in fertility. In women fertility declines to zero after menopause.

KEY TERMS: Mix and Match (page 277)

acrosome reaction (X), apoptosis (K), blastocyst (O), breast (B), childbirth (=parturition or labor) (I), cortical reaction (N), degenerative disease (M), endometrium (U), estrogen (L), fertility (D), fertilization (R), FSH (A), implantation (Q), lactation (BB), LH (Z), menopause (T), menstrual cycle (H), oogenesis (S), oxytocin (F), placenta (AA), pregnancy (J), progesterone (P), prostaglandins (Y), puberty (C), reproductive system (E), spermatogenesis (W), STI (V), testosterone (G).